Antony Worrall Thompson's
WEEKEND COOKBOOK

Antony's
WEEKEND COOKBOOK

Compiled and edited by Orla Broderick

BBC
BOOKS

GoodFood
magazine

To Michael Kelpie and all his team on
Saturday Cooks, who start my weekends
off with a bang.

**Specially commissioned photography
by Steve Lee**

1 3 5 7 9 10 8 6 4 2

Published in 2006 by BBC Books,
an imprint of Ebury Publishing

Ebury Publishing is a division of the Random House Group

Copyright © Antony Worrall Thompson 2006

Antony Worrall Thompson has asserted his right to be identified as
the author of this Work in accordance with the Copyright, Designs
and Patents Act 1988

The Random House Group Limited Reg. No. 954009

Addresses for companies within the Random House Group can be found
at www.randomhouse.co.uk

A CIP catalogue record for this book is available from the British Library

The Random House Group Limited makes every effort to ensure that the
papers used in our books are made from trees that have been legally
sourced from well-managed and credibly certified forests. Our paper
procurement policy can be found at www.randomhouse.co.uk

Colour printing by CPI Bath
Colour separations by Dot Gradations Ltd, UK

ISBN 0 563 49380 1
ISBN (from January 2007) 978 0 563 49380 8

All photography by Steve Lee © BBC Books 2006, except those on pages
2–3, 9, 30, 35, 55, 73, 94, 112, 113, 134, 136, 137, 138, 139, 141, 142, 143,
147, 152, 153 and 156, which were taken by Lisa Linder © BBC
Worldwide 2006 and which first appeared in *BBC Good Food Magazine*

A proportion of these recipes have appeared previously in *Saturday
Kitchen Cookbook* (BBC Books 2004), *Antony Worrall Thompson's Top 100
Beef Recipes* (BBC Books 2005), *The Top 100 Recipes from Food and Drink*
(BBC Books 2005) and *BBC Good Food Magazine*

CONTENTS

Anto

ny's

INTRODUCTION

Weekends – everyone's favourite time of the week, unless of course you happen to be working. But for most people it's a time of relaxation, a time to enjoy the family, a time for fun, and a time for enjoying some good food without the midweek rush.

After I finish my Saturday morning TV show, I love to rush off to a farmers' market to see what's on offer, to look at great local produce and to continue my new found love of eating with the seasons. I don't know about you, but I'm getting fed up with eating strawberries all year round and bored with eating asparagus with no flavour when I know how wonderful English asparagus can be, even if it does only have a six-week season. It's time to get back to seasonal eating – it makes sense eating summery salads and vegetables in the summer and earthy roots during the winter. And in this book you'll find a variety of seasonal recipes.

Weekends are the time when people cook. It's a disappointing but true fact that fewer and fewer adults are cooking during the week. And yet come the weekend, there are a whole host of people getting stuck into cookery as a leisure activity, a hobby if you wish. And what I've noticed from the demonstrations I give, is that there's some gender bending going on in the kitchen – more and more men are enjoying the 'feminine' art of cooking. Cooking should be relaxing, it should be fun and nowadays, I'm afraid to say, there is no point in cooking if you're not enjoying it, with the convenience on offer through ready meals, take-aways and eating out.

But for those of you who watch us TV chefs working our craft, if we make you feel insecure about your abilities, forget it, chill a little. We make cooking look easy because it is easy. Cooking well is all about confidence – the more you do it, the easier it becomes – and with confidence comes the ability to veer off the straight and narrow. Have even more fun by chucking in a little of this, removing a little of that. Recipes are merely guidelines. They are created to individual tastebuds, which may not satisfy everyone.

Weekends offer so many options for meal-time experiences, from lazy breakfasts to an American-style brunch, from having a few mates over for a relaxing Saturday lunch before the big game to more formal Saturday-evening dining where you make just a tad more effort. Then on to that compulsory meal of the week, the classic Sunday roast, but should you not have time for that I've provided you with some easy family suppers. And should the weather be kind to you there's even barbecue and picnic food to choose from.

None of the dishes in my book is complicated or difficult to achieve. This is food that I enjoy cooking and eating, food I love to share with family and friends. As much as I enjoy you eating in my or other peoples' restaurants, you get so much more pleasure and so much more relaxation by dining in your own surroundings. You can take your time, you don't have to leave and if that is your wont, you can sit back and enjoy a bevvy or two without worrying about who is going to drive home!

Writing this book has given me a lot of fun and enjoyment. I hope it provides you with as much pleasure.

Antony Worrall Thompson

saturday breakfasts

The Classics

Beef hash browns

The Full Monty breakfast

Hot-smoked salmon kedgeree

New Twists

Asparagus custards

'Hambled' eggs on toasted muffins

Smoked haddock and potato cakes with poached eggs

Baked herby tomatoes

Perfect for Kids

Apple pancakes with pork sausages

Quick quesadillas

Bacon and banana torpedoes

Sweet Nothings

Blackberry burnt cream

Mango and passion fruit smoothie

Brioche pain perdu with smashed raspberry cream

One of my favourite things to have for breakfast Stateside.
The secret to a good hash is to keep breaking up the mixture
and stirring the brown, crispy bits into the centre of the pan.
Traditionally it is made with salt or pickled beef; I have
adapted this recipe to use minced beef.

Beef hash browns

50 g (2 oz) unsalted butter
450 g (1 lb) minced beef
*4 rindless smoked streaky bacon rashers, finely
  chopped*
4 ripe tomatoes, peeled, seeded and chopped
1 onion, finely chopped
2 garlic cloves, finely chopped
2 tbsp sherry vinegar
1 tbsp Dijon mustard

*450 g (1 lb) potatoes, grated (a floury, starchy
  variety is best)*
*50 g (2 oz) beef dripping (fat from roasted meat)
  or 4 tbsp olive oil*
olive oil, for cooking
4–6 small ripe tomatoes, cut in half
4–6 eggs
Worcestershire sauce, to taste
salt and freshly ground black pepper

Melt the butter in a small pan or in the microwave. Transfer to a large
bowl and add the minced beef, bacon, tomatoes, onion, garlic, sherry
vinegar, Dijon mustard and potatoes. Season to taste and, using your
hands, mix well to combine.

Heat a heavy-based frying pan. Add the beef dripping or olive oil, then
tip in the beef mixture and cook over a high heat for about 10 minutes,
stirring frequently.

Reduce the heat and cook for another 10 minutes until the potatoes are
completely tender and the hash is brown and crispy all over.

Meanwhile, heat a griddle pan and large frying pan. Add a thin layer
of olive oil to each one, then add the tomatoes to the griddle pan, cut-side
down, and cook for 6–8 minutes until lightly charred and heated through,
turning once. Remove from the pan and keep warm. Break the eggs into
the frying pan and gently fry for a couple of minutes, spooning a little of
the hot oil over the yolks, until they are just set.

Season the cooked beef hash brown with the Worcestershire sauce and
divide among warmed plates. Arrange the chargrilled tomatoes alongside
and finish each one with a fried egg to serve.

How often have we all made this when there's a crowd to feed in the house? Well, it's actually not as easy as it looks and needs a bit of clever timing if the results are going to be perfect. Don't be tempted to prick the sausages – you want all of the flavour to stay inside the skin.

The Full Monty breakfast

SERVES 4

4 ripe beef tomatoes

olive oil and knob butter, for cooking

1 small onion, finely chopped

1 garlic clove, finely chopped

175 g (6 oz) flat or field mushrooms, chopped

$^1/_2$ tsp fresh thyme leaves

4–8 pork sausages

8–12 rindless smoked streaky bacon rashers

4 slices day-old rustic or ciabatta bread

4 eggs

salt and freshly ground black pepper

Preheat the oven to 200°C/400°F/Gas 6 and preheat the grill. Slice the top off each tomato and, being careful not to damage the outer skin, scoop out the seeds with a teaspoon, then sprinkle the insides with a little salt. Turn the tomatoes upside down and allow any excess juices to drain away.

Meanwhile, heat one tablespoon of olive oil in a large frying pan and gently cook the onion and garlic for 2–3 minutes until softened but not coloured. Add another tablespoon of olive oil and the mushrooms to the pan and cook over a high heat for a couple of minutes until they start to wilt. Fold in the thyme and season to taste.

Arrange the tomato cases in a lightly greased small baking dish. Fill with the onion and mushroom mixture and replace the tops of the tomatoes. Drizzle over a little olive oil and roast for 15–20 minutes until the tomatoes have softened but not split.

Arrange the sausages on a grill rack and cook for 15–20 minutes, turning regularly until dark brown all over.

Wipe out the frying pan, add a teaspoon or two of oil and fry the bacon for 1–2 minutes on each side until crisp and golden brown. Put on to a baking sheet and keep warm. Heat another tablespoon of oil with the bacon fat left in the frying pan, add the bread slices and fry for 1–2 minutes on each side until crisp and golden. Add to the baking sheet to keep warm.

Wipe the frying pan clean again, heat a thin layer of oil over a medium heat with the knob of butter and fry the eggs, spooning a little of the hot fat over the yolks, until they are just set. To serve, arrange the tomatoes on warmed plates with the sausages, bacon, fried bread and fried eggs.

Kedgeree originated in India where the leftover rice and fish from the previous evening's meal were mixed together with ghee and served for breakfast. This version uses hot-smoked salmon but it is also wonderful made with smoked haddock that has been poached in a little fish stock.

Hot-smoked salmon kedgeree

SERVES 4

225 g (8 oz) basmati rice
400 ml (14 fl oz) fish stock
2 eggs
50 g (2 oz) unsalted butter
1 small onion, finely chopped
5 cm (2 in) fresh root ginger, peeled and finely
  chopped

1 tsp medium curry paste
350 g (12 oz) hot-smoked salmon
2 tbsp double cream (optional)
2 tbsp chopped fresh flat-leaf parsley
salt and freshly ground black pepper

Rinse the rice in one or two changes of water to get rid of some of the surface starch. Bring the fish stock and rice to the boil in a pan with a tight-fitting lid, then turn the heat down to an absolute minimum. Cover and cook for 15 minutes, then remove from the heat and leave undisturbed for another 5 minutes to steam.

Meanwhile, cook the eggs in a small pan of simmering water for 7–8 minutes until nearly hard-boiled. Rinse under cold water and crack away the shell, then roughly chop.

Heat half the butter in a large pan, then add the onion and ginger and cook over a gentle heat for 2–3 minutes until the onion has softened but not coloured. Stir in the curry paste and cook for another 2 minutes, stirring continuously. Fold in the rice and cook until warmed through, tossing the pan occasionally.

Skin the hot-smoked salmon and then flake the flesh. Gently fold into the flavoured rice with the cream, if using, and the hard-boiled eggs. To finish the kedgeree, stir in the remaining butter with the parsley and season to taste. Transfer to a warmed dish and serve while still hot.

These are basically savoury crème caramels with a delicate and fresh summer flavour. I would serve these if we had friends to stay for the weekend and probably do something different for the children, such as the Quick Quesadillas (page 25).

Asparagus custards

SERVES 4

25 g (1 oz) unsalted butter

225 g (8 oz) asparagus spears, trimmed

450 ml (^{3}/$_4$ pint) double cream

1 garlic clove, crushed

1 tsp snipped fresh chives

1 tsp chopped fresh chervil

2 tsp chopped fresh flat-leaf parsley

4 eggs

salt and freshly ground white pepper

lightly dressed rocket salad, to serve

Preheat the oven to 150°C/300°F/Gas 2. Butter 4 x 150 ml (^{1}/$_4$ pint) ramekins. Cut the tips from the asparagus to a length of 4 cm (1^1/$_2$ in), then cut each tip into four lengthways and set aside. Slice the remaining asparagus stems and plunge into a pan of boiling water for 2 minutes, then drain and quickly refresh under cold running water to prevent further cooking.

Place the cream in a pan with the garlic and boil until reduced to 300 ml (^{1}/$_2$ pint) in total, stirring occasionally. Transfer to a food processor and add the blanched asparagus and all the herbs. Blend until smooth.

Break the eggs into a bowl and lightly whisk, then stir in the cream mixture until well combined. Season to taste and strain through a fine sieve into a jug.

Divide the reserved asparagus tips between the ramekins, then carefully pour in the cream mixture. Transfer to a roasting tin and pour in enough boiling water to come halfway up the sides of the ramekins. Bake for 35–40 minutes until the custards are just set but still have a slight wobble in the centre. Remove from the oven and leave to stand for 5 minutes, then invert on to plates. Add a little dressed rocket to each plate to serve, if liked.

If you are in a bit of a hurry to leave the house but want to have something substantial before going out, then these ham-scrambled eggs are the perfect way to start the day.

'Hambled' eggs on toasted muffins

SERVES 4

8 eggs

pinch salt

pinch cayenne pepper

85 g (3 oz) unsalted butter

2 white muffins, split in half

225 g (8 oz) cooked ham slices, trimmed
   and cut into small pieces

1 tsp snipped fresh chives

Preheat the grill. Break the eggs into a bowl and season to taste with salt and cayenne pepper. Beat together lightly with a fork. Melt 50 g (2 oz) of the butter in a large non-stick pan, swirling it around so that it coats the sides. Add the eggs and cook over a low heat for 2–3 minutes until the eggs are half set, stirring continuously.

Meanwhile, arrange the muffin halves on a grill pan, cut-side up, and cook for 2–3 minutes until lightly toasted. Spread with the remaining butter.

Remove the egg mixture from the heat and add the ham, then return to the heat briefly and continue to stir until the eggs are soft and creamy. Arrange the muffins on warmed plates and spoon the 'hambled' eggs on top. Sprinkle over the chives to serve.

I could never tire of a plate of fish cakes as a late Saturday breakfast. In my mind it's one of the great British classics. The main ingredients always stay the same but this is a version that works particularly well with the poached eggs.

Smoked haddock and potato cakes with poached eggs

350 g (12 oz) potatoes, cut into chunks
225 g (8 oz) haddock fillet (in one piece)
175 g (6 oz) undyed smoked haddock fillet (in one piece)
300 ml (¹/₂ pint) milk
1 bay leaf
few peppercorns
85 g (3 oz) unsalted butter

1 small onion, finely chopped
2 tsp anchovy essence
2 tbsp chopped fresh mixed herbs (such as flat-leaf parsley, dill and chives)
1 tbsp white wine vinegar
4 eggs
25 g (1 oz) seasoned plain flour
salt and freshly ground black pepper

Place the potatoes in a pan of boiling salted water, cover and cook for 15–20 minutes until tender. Drain and return to the pan for a couple of minutes to dry out, then mash well.

Place the fish fillets in a frying pan with a lid. Add the milk, bay leaf and peppercorns, then cover and bring to a simmer. Poach for a few minutes until both haddocks are just tender. Transfer to a plate with a fish slice and flake, discarding any skin and bones.

Heat 25 g (1 oz) of the butter in a frying pan and sweat the onion for about 5 minutes until softened, then add 25 g (1 oz) of the butter and just allow to melt. Tip into a bowl and add the cooked potatoes, flaked fish, anchovy essence and herbs, then mix well. Season to taste, then shape the fish mixture into four patties and arrange on a baking sheet. Chill for at least 2 hours or up to 24 hours to firm up.

Heat a large pan with 2.25 litres (4 pints) water. Add the white wine vinegar and bring to the boil. Break each egg into the water where it is bubbling, then move the pan to the edge of the heat and simmer gently for 2 minutes. Remove the eggs with a slotted spoon and plunge into a bowl of iced water. When cold, trim down any ragged ends from the cooked egg white and discard. The eggs will keep happily in the fridge for up to 24 hours.

When ready to cook, heat the remaining butter in a frying pan. Dust the fish patties in the seasoned flour and add to the pan, then cook for

5–10 minutes on each side until heated through and golden brown.

Bring a large pan of salted water to the boil. Add the poached eggs and cook for 1 minute to warm through. Place a smoked haddock and potato cake on each warmed plate. Using a slotted spoon, remove the poached eggs from the pan and drain briefly on kitchen paper. Put one on each fish cake to serve.

Serve these tasty stuffed tomatoes on their own or, for a
more substantial breakfast, with crispy Parma ham and
creamy scrambled eggs. Look in your local supermarket
for the tomatoes that have been specially grown for flavour,
such as Jack Hawkins, which is one of my favourite varieties.
(What did they used to be grown for? It makes you wonder ...)

Baked herby tomatoes

SERVES 4

4 ripe, firm, large tomatoes

1 shallot, finely diced

2 garlic cloves, finely chopped

1 tsp fresh thyme leaves

2 tbsp extra-virgin olive oil

4 anchovy fillets, drained and finely chopped

2 tbsp roughly chopped fresh flat-leaf parsley

$^1/_2$ tsp dried chilli flakes

50 g (2 oz) fresh white breadcrumbs

salt and freshly ground black pepper

extra-virgin olive oil and balsamic vinegar,
   to garnish

Cut the tomatoes in half horizontally and carefully remove the seeds
with a teaspoon. Sprinkle the cut sides with salt and place cut-side down
on kitchen paper to remove some liquid. Leave to stand for 20 minutes.

Preheat the oven to 200°C/400°F/Gas 6. Place the shallot in a food
processor with the garlic, thyme, olive oil and anchovies and then blend
to a smooth paste. Transfer to a bowl and fold in the parsley, chilli flakes
and breadcrumbs until well combined. Season to taste.

Spoon the bread mixture into the tomato cavities and bake for about
15 minutes until bubbling and golden brown. Transfer to a dish and serve
hot or at room temperature drizzled with the extra-virgin olive oil and
balsamic vinegar.

I am a big fan of Bramley cooking apples and these pancakes are a novel way of using them for breakfast. Buy the best, meatiest pork sausages you can find and don't be tempted to prick them while they are cooking or those lovely juices will come flowing out.

Apple pancakes with pork sausages

SERVES 4

8 large pork sausages
175 g (6 oz) plain flour
1 tsp baking powder
¹/₂ tsp ground cinnamon
about 40 g (1¹/₂ oz) unsalted butter

1 tbsp caster sugar
2 eggs, beaten
1 large cooking apple, peeled, cored and
    finely chopped
300 ml (¹/₂ pint) milk
sunflower oil, for cooking

Preheat a griddle pan over a medium heat until very hot. Add the sausages and cook for 10–15 minutes until cooked through and lightly charred, turning once.

Meanwhile, make the apple pancakes. Heat a large heavy-based pan. Sift the flour, baking powder and cinnamon into a bowl. Using a wooden spoon, cream together 15 g (¹/₂ oz) of the butter and the sugar in a separate bowl until light and fluffy. Beat in the eggs, adding a little of the flour mixture to prevent the mixture from curdling. Fold in the rest of the flour mixture and then stir in the chopped apple. Gradually add the milk, stirring until smooth after each addition until you have achieved a batter.

Add a thin film of oil to the heated pan and then add a little of the remaining butter. Once the butter has melted, ladle in spoonfuls of the pancake batter, allowing them to spread out to no more than 7.5 cm (3 in) in diameter. Reduce the heat and cook for 2–3 minutes until small bubbles appear on the surface.

Turn the pancakes over and cook for another 1–2 minutes until the pancakes are lightly golden. Stack on a plate and keep warm, then repeat until you have 12 pancakes in total. Arrange three pancakes on each warmed plate with the chargrilled sausages and serve at once.

These quesadilla triangles are addictive, and make the perfect late breakfast for the whole family. They can be prepared up to one hour in advance, covered with cling film and kept at room temperature. Simply flash through the oven when you are ready to serve.

Quick quesadillas

SERVES 4

8 soft flour tortillas
2 tbsp olive oil, for brushing
225 g (8 oz) Cheddar, grated
1 mild red chilli, seeded and finely
  chopped

4 spring onions, finely chopped
about 120 ml (4 fl oz) soured cream or
  thick Greek yoghurt
good handful fresh coriander leaves
salt and freshly ground black pepper
salsa, to serve (optional)

Preheat the oven to 200°C/400°F/Gas 6 and heat a griddle pan over a medium heat until very hot. Brush one side of each tortilla with a little of the olive oil. Place one tortilla in the pan, oiled-side down, and cook for 1 minute until nicely marked, pressing down with a spatula. Repeat with the remaining tortillas.

Arrange half the tortillas on baking sheets, marked-side down. Sprinkle over the cheese and then scatter the chilli and spring onions on top. Season to taste. Cover with the remaining tortillas, marked-side up, and bake for about 5 minutes or until heated through and the cheese has melted. Allow to cool slightly until easy to handle.

Cut each quesadilla into eight wedges with a serrated knife, pizza cutter or kitchen scissors. Garnish each wedge with a small spoonful of soured cream or yoghurt and a coriander leaf. Arrange on warmed plates or one large platter to serve, with a separate bowl of salsa to hand around, if liked.

This is a winning sandwich for children – and, if I'm honest, the adults in our house, too. These are great to eat in the car if you are planning an early start for a day trip, and as bananas are an excellent source of slow-releasing carbohydrate they should keep everyone happy until lunchtime. Add a little yoghurt or butter to the rolls, if you like.

Bacon and banana torpedoes

SERVES 4

*8 rindless streaky
    bacon rashers*
4 firm ripe bananas
4 white soft hot-dog rolls

Preheat the grill. Using a table knife, stretch each bacon rasher, being careful not to tear them. Peel the bananas and wrap two bacon rashers round each one, tucking in the ends to make sure that they will stay in place.

Arrange the bacon-wrapped bananas on a grill rack and cook for about 10 minutes until the bacon is crisp and golden and the banana is softening, turning occasionally.

Split the rolls and slap a bacon-wrapped banana into each one. Wrap the bottom half in a napkin and serve immediately.

Use any berries for this dish; blackberries are a particular favourite of mine in the autumn. We go picking them early in the morning and then come back for a leisurely breakfast.

Blackberry burnt cream

SERVES 4

225 g (8 oz) blackberries
*250 g (9 oz) thick
    Greek yoghurt*
*4 tbsp caster sugar
    (golden, if possible)*

Preheat the grill to high. Fill 4 × 150 ml ($^1/_4$ pint) ramekins with the blackberries. Cover with a layer of the Greek yoghurt and smooth over the top with a flat knife.

Sprinkle an even layer of caster sugar over each one, completely covering the yoghurt, and arrange on a sturdy baking sheet. Place under the hot grill for 30 seconds to 1 minute or until the sugar has just melted and caramelized – you could also use a mini blowtorch for this. Allow the sugar to cool and set for a minute or so before serving.

For me, breakfast in a glass is the perfect way to start the day. If the fruit is nice and ripe I find there's no need to sweeten with sugar and honey, but that of course is personal preference.

Mango and passion fruit smoothie

SERVES 4

1 ripe large mango, peeled, flesh cut away from the stone
2 passion fruit, halved and juice rubbed through a sieve
1 ripe large banana, peeled and roughly chopped
juice 1 lime
300 ml ($^1/_2$ pint) freshly squeezed orange juice
250 g (9 oz) thick Greek yoghurt
175 g (6 oz) ice cubes

Place the mango in a liquidizer with the passion fruit juice, banana, lime juice, orange juice, yoghurt and ice cubes. Blend until smooth. Alternatively, you can put everything into a large measuring jug and blend with a hand-held blender, moving it up and down, until smooth. Pour into tumbler glasses to serve.

Bionic Berry
Place 450 g (1 lb) frozen mixed berries into the liquidizer with the finely grated rind and juice of 1 lemon and add the same quantities of orange juice and yoghurt as above. Blend until smooth and pour into tumbler glasses to serve.

Tropical Fruit
Place 450 g (1 lb) frozen tropical fruit into the liquidizer with the juice of 1 lime, 400 g (14 oz) can of coconut milk and 300 ml ($^1/_2$ pint) tropical fruit juice or freshly squeezed orange juice. Blend until smooth and pour into tumbler glasses to serve.

Kiwi Crush
Peel and slice 2 ripe kiwi and place in a liquidizer with 4 tablespoons of elderflower cordial and 600 ml (1 pint) grapefruit juice. Add 175 g (6 oz) ice cubes and blend until smooth, then pour into tall glasses to serve.

This is my version of pain perdu, French toast or eggy bread, call it what you will. They are all different names for the same breakfast indulgence. Change the fruit you serve with it as the seasons change – fried apples for the autumn, buttery bananas for winter and perhaps fresh blueberries for spring.

Brioche pain perdu with smashed raspberry cream

SERVES 4

120 ml (4 fl oz) double cream
100 g (4 oz) raspberries
3 eggs
120 ml (4 fl oz) milk
120 ml (4 fl oz) single cream

good pinch ground cinnamon
few drops vanilla extract
2 tsp caster sugar
25 g (1 oz) unsalted butter
4 thick slices day-old brioche or country
  bread

Whip the double cream in a bowl until soft peaks form. Roughly mash the raspberries in a separate bowl and then gently fold into the cream to create a ripple effect. Cover with cling film and chill until needed.

Beat the eggs in a shallow dish with the milk, single cream, a pinch of the cinnamon and the vanilla extract to a smooth batter. Combine the caster sugar with the remaining cinnamon in a small bowl and set aside.

Heat the butter in a frying pan. Soak the brioche or country bread slices in the egg mixture for 2 minutes, turning once. Carefully lift into the pan and cook for 2 minutes on each side or until golden brown.

Arrange the pain perdu on warmed plates and spoon the smashed raspberry cream on top. Sprinkle with the cinnamon sugar to serve.

a luxurious breakfast-time treat

deli-style lunches

Summery Salads

Mango, crab and avocado salad

Broad bean and Brie salad

Cucumber salad with soured cream and dill

Sweet peppers stuffed with brandade

Lunch on the Go

Celeriac remoulade

Roast carrot and beetroot salad with goats' cheese

Warm salad of chickpeas and chorizo

Melted Vacherin Mont d'Or with various accompaniments

American club sandwich

Soup-kitchen Specials

Roast swede soup with Crozier blue croutons

Beetroot soup with horseradish

Chicken noodle soup

This is great for a hot summer's day. It should be chilled for
at least an hour before serving so it is perfect if you're
having a couple of people over for a light lunch.

Mango, crab and avocado salad

SERVES 4
225 g (8 oz) fresh white crabmeat
1 ripe large mango
200 ml (7 fl oz) soured cream

2 shallots, finely chopped
2 tsp fresh lemon juice
4 tsp brandy
$^1/_4$ tsp sweet paprika
1 large Little Gem lettuce

4 ripe avocados
salt and freshly ground black
  pepper
tiny cherry tomatoes and fresh
  dill sprigs, to garnish

Using two forks, shred the crabmeat, discarding any pieces of shell.
Place in a bowl. Peel the mango and then cut away the flesh from the
stone before finely chopping. Add to the crab and fold together.

Add the soured cream to the crab mixture with the shallots, lemon juice,
brandy and paprika, and season to taste. Stir until well combined.

Separate the Little Gem lettuce into individual leaves and use to cover
a large platter. Cut the avocados in half and remove the stones, then
carefully peel away the skin. Fill with the crab mixture and arrange on
the lettuce leaves.

Chill the mango, crab and avocado salad for at least 1 hour or up to 2; any
longer and the avocados are in danger of discolouring. Garnish the platter
with the cherry tomatoes and dill sprigs, and allow guests to help themselves.

Few things taste better than a dish of young tender broad beans, lovingly cooked. They are one of the first vegetables we gardeners get to feast on in early spring and are always in the shops by mid-May or early June. Otherwise most supermarkets sell them frozen.

Broad bean and Brie salad

SERVES 4

675 g (1¹/₂ lb) fresh broad
    beans in their pods
4 tbsp extra-virgin olive oil

finely grated rind and juice
    1 lemon
4 tbsp chopped fresh flat-leaf
    parsley

350 g (12 oz) ripe Brie cheese
salt and freshly ground black
    pepper
crusty French bread, to serve

Shell the broad beans. Bring a large pan of salted water to the boil and cook the beans for 2–3 minutes until just tender. Drain and quickly refresh under cold running water to prevent further cooking, then slip the bright green beans out of their tough inner skins.

Tip the broad beans into a bowl and dress with the extra-virgin olive oil, lemon rind and juice, and season to taste. Toss well to combine and then stir in the parsley.

Divide the dressed broad beans between plates. Cut the Brie into twelve wedges and place three on top of each portion of the beans. Serve at once with crusty bread, if liked.

This is a light summery salad that goes well with smoked salmon or trout. It would also be delicious with poached fish, such as sea bass or salmon.

Cucumber salad with soured cream and dill

SERVES 4

2 cucumbers

2 tbsp cider vinegar

2 tsp caster sugar

150 ml ($^1/_4$ pint) soured cream or crème fraiche

4 spring onions, thinly sliced

small bunch fresh chives, snipped

small bunch fresh dill, snipped

large pinch celery seeds (optional)

salt and freshly ground black pepper

pinch paprika, to serve

Cut the cucumbers in half and run a teaspoon down the middle of each piece to scoop out the seeds, then thinly slice on the diagonal. Place in a bowl and sprinkle over a teaspoon of salt with half of the vinegar and sugar, tossing to coat. Tip into a sieve and put back over the bowl. Set aside for 30 minutes, then gently squeeze between sheets of kitchen roll to remove excess juices.

Place the soured cream or crème fraiche in a bowl with the remaining vinegar and sugar. Add the spring onions, with most of the chives, dill and celery seeds, if using. Season to taste, fold in the cucumber and sprinkle with a dusting of paprika. Garnish with the remaining herbs to serve.

Salt cod is now readily available. It needs to be soaked for an hour or so if only lightly salted, or up to 24 hours if very dried out. To make your own, cover a fillet of cod with a thick layer of salt and chill for 24 hours – this will keep for up to a week covered with cling film in the fridge.

Sweet peppers stuffed with brandade

SERVES 4

225 g (8 oz) salt cod, soaked
* (see above)*
225 ml (8 fl oz) olive oil
225 ml (8 fl oz) double cream
4 garlic cloves, roughly chopped

freshly ground white pepper
375 g (13 oz) jar whole sweet piquante
* peppers*
ciabatta, to serve
chopped fresh flat-leaf parsley, to garnish

Poach the cod in a shallow pan in a little water for about 10 minutes, then drain and flake the flesh into a food processor, removing the skin and bones.

Place the olive oil and cream in a separate pan and bring to the boil. Add the garlic to the flaked salt cod and turn the food processor on. Gradually pour in the hot oil and cream mixture through the feeder tube to form a thick emulsion. Season with white pepper and use to fill the peppers, then arrange on plates with the ciabatta. Garnish with the parsley to serve.

Choose the smoothest-looking celeriac you can find for this classic French salad. It's a good idea to cut it into quarters before you start peeling it so you can see exactly what you are doing and avoid waste.

Celeriac remoulade

SERVES 4
1 small celeriac
1 lemon
6 tbsp mayonnaise
4 tbsp double cream

4 tsp Dijon mustard
salt and freshly ground black pepper
chopped fresh flat-leaf parsley, to garnish
slices Parma ham, bowl of olives and
    crusty French bread, to serve

Cut the celeriac into quarters and then peel each piece. Cut the lemon in half and use one half to rub all over the celeriac to prevent discolouration. Quickly cut the celeriac into julienne strips using a mandolin or with the shredder attachment of your food processor. Place in a bowl and squeeze over the remaining half of the lemon to prevent discolouration, tossing to coat.

Place the mayonnaise in a large bowl with the cream and mustard. Season to taste and then stir well to combine. Fold in the celeriac julienne and pile on to a platter. Place in the fridge for a couple of hours for the flavours to develop, then garnish with the parsley to serve. Allow guests to help themselves to the salad and have it with the Parma ham, olives and some crusty French bread.

I eat this salad with slices of rare roast beef for a more substantial lunch. Use any selection of salad leaves you have to hand – my preference would be a mixture of baby spinach, wild rocket and watercress sprigs.

Roast carrot and beetroot salad with goats' cheese

SERVES 4

200 g (7 oz) baby beetroot, scrubbed clean

3 tbsp olive oil

225 g (8 oz) carrots, cut into 3 cm (1¹/₄ in) chunks

2 garlic cloves

2 tbsp sherry vinegar

6 tbsp extra-virgin olive oil

200 g (7 oz) green salad leaves

good pinch fresh thyme leaves

225 g (8 oz) young goats' cheese, sliced or crumbled

salt and freshly ground black pepper

slices rare roast beef, to serve (optional)

Preheat the oven to 200°C/400°F/Gas 6. Place the beetroot in a roasting tin, season generously and drizzle over the olive oil. Roast for 30 minutes, then add the carrots and garlic to the tin, tossing to coat in the oil. Return to the oven for another 15 minutes until the carrots are tender but retain a bit of bite, turning occasionally.

Remove the baby beetroot from the tin and allow to cool slightly before squeezing out of their skins. Place in a bowl with the roasted carrots, discarding the garlic.

To make the dressing, deglaze the roasting tin on the hob with the sherry vinegar. Pass through a fine sieve into a bowl and whisk in the extra-virgin olive oil. Season to taste. Gently fold in the salad leaves with the thyme and goats' cheese, tossing until evenly coated. Divide between plates to serve with the rare roast beef, if liked.

This salad is a wonderful combination of flavours and textures that is incredibly simple to prepare. I like to serve it warm, but it would also be good at room temperature, especially as part of a feast. Where possible buy the raw cooking chorizo rather than the salami-style chorizo.

Warm salad of chickpeas and chorizo

SERVES 4

3 tbsp olive oil

3 red chillies, seeded and thinly sliced

12 garlic cloves, chopped

3 red onions, thinly sliced

150 ml (¼ pint) cider vinegar

8 mini chorizos, sliced in half lengthways

2 x 400 g (14 oz) cans chickpeas, drained
  and rinsed

1 large handful fresh coriander leaves,
  roughly chopped

1 large handful fresh flat-leaf parsley
  leaves

1 large handful fresh mint leaves

225 g (8 oz) feta cheese, chopped

8 spring onions, thinly sliced

3 tbsp extra-virgin olive oil

salt and freshly ground black pepper

Heat two tablespoons of the olive oil in a pan. Add the chillies, garlic and red onions and cook over a high heat for 5 minutes, stirring quite frequently to prevent the mixture from sticking. Pour in the vinegar and boil fast for about 2 minutes until it has evaporated. Transfer to a large bowl and leave to sit for 15 minutes before giving it another stir. Season to taste.

Heat the remaining olive oil in the frying pan and add the mini chorizos. Fry for a few minutes to release the fats, then add the chickpeas and continue to cook for a few minutes until the mini chorizos are cooked through. Tip into the chilli mixture and toss until well combined.

Fold the herbs into the salad with the feta cheese and spring onions, and dress with the extra-virgin olive oil, tossing until well coated. Season to taste and divide between plates to serve.

Vacherin Mont d'Or is a fantastic Swiss cheese made in the Jura mountains from unpasteurized cows' milk. It is a winter cheese that is not available in the spring or summer, which is why I've given the alternative of Camembert.

Melted Vacherin Mont d'Or with various accompaniments

SERVES 4

1 wheel Vacherin Mont d'Or or Camembert (in a wooden box)
1 garlic clove, cut into 6 slices (optional)
6 spriglets fresh thyme
350 g (12 oz) baby new potatoes

1 small ciabatta, cut into chunks
100 g (4 oz) drained gherkins
225 g (8 oz) selection of charcuterie, such as salami, prosciutto and smoked duck slices (optional)
salt and freshly ground black pepper

Preheat the oven to 230°C/450°F/Gas 8. Remove the wrapper from the Vacherin Mont d'Or or Camembert and return it to its wooden box. Make six deep cuts in the surface of the cheese and push a slice of garlic, if using, and a spriglet of thyme into each one. Wrap the cheese and its box in foil and place in the oven for 20–30 minutes, depending on how ripe the cheese is, until completely melted and warmed through.

Meanwhile, cook the potatoes in a covered pan of boiling salted water for 15–20 minutes or until tender.

When the cheese is ready, carefully unwrap the foil and place the box in the centre of a deep platter. Pile the boiled potatoes, ciabatta and gherkins round the cheese, with the selection of charcuterie in overlapping layers to one side, if using. Season to taste and serve at once.

I like to use leftover roast chicken in this sandwich, but if you haven't got any to hand try the egg, pistachio and basil instead, omitting the avocado and chives. This needs to be made just before it's eaten, otherwise the fried bread begins to harden.

American club sandwich

SERVES 2
2 tbsp olive oil
6 slices rindless streaky bacon rashers
6 slices country-style bread
4 tbsp mayonnaise
1 small Little Gem lettuce, separated into leaves
100 g (4 oz) cooked chicken, sliced

1 ripe avocado, peeled, stoned and sliced
1 tbsp snipped fresh chives
$^1/_2$ cucumber, sliced
2 plum tomatoes, sliced
salt and freshly ground black pepper
crinkle-cut crisps, to serve

Heat a large frying pan. Add a tablespoon of olive oil and cook the bacon for 1–2 minutes on each side until crisp and golden. Transfer to kitchen paper to crisp up and add the remaining tablespoon of olive oil to the pan. Add four slices of the bread and fry for a few minutes on one side until golden brown.

Lay the four fried slices, crispy side down, and the remaining two fresh slices of bread on the work surface. Spread with the mayonnaise.

Top two of the fried slices with the Little Gem lettuce leaves and then scatter the chicken, avocado and chives over them. Top this with the uncooked slices of bread, and then add the cucumber, bacon and tomatoes. Season to taste. Cover with the remaining bread slices, fried-face up. Secure each sandwich with two cocktail sticks and slice in half. Arrange on plates with crisps to the side.

Egg, Pistachio and Basil
Chop four hard-boiled eggs and combine in a bowl with 2 tablespoons chopped pistachio nuts, 3 tablespoons soured cream, 1 teaspoon Dijon mustard, 12 ripped fresh basil leaves and season with salt and a pinch of paprika. Use to fill two split granary rolls.

Piquant Prawn
Place 100 g (4 oz) cooked peeled prawns in a food processor with 50 g (2 oz) unsalted butter, 1 teaspoon anchovy essence, a dash of Tabasco sauce and a squeeze of lemon juice. Blend to a paste. Season to taste and spread on

slices of lightly buttered wholemeal bread. Cut into triangles and garnish with watercress.

My Favourite Sandwich

Cook four slices of rindless streaky bacon in a little olive oil until crispy. Spread two slices of wholemeal bread with 50 g (2 oz) cream cheese and arrange 100 g (4 oz) smoked salmon slices on top. Sprinkle over 2 teaspoons finely chopped red onion and drizzle over a little mango chutney that has been let down with a drop of water. Top with the crispy bacon and 1 teaspoon small capers. Finish the open sandwiches with a dusting of snipped chives and freshly ground black pepper.

Keep an eye out for Crozier blue, a fantastic sheep's cheese
from County Tipperary, in your local deli. If you can't find it,
use Gorgonzola or Cashel blue. This soup freezes brilliantly
so can be made well in advance and thawed out when needed.

Roast swede soup with Crozier blue croutons

SERVES 4

1 swede, peeled and cut into cubes

3 tbsp olive oil

1 onion, finely chopped

2 carrots, finely chopped

2 celery stalks, finely chopped

1 garlic clove, crushed

1 tsp chopped fresh thyme

1.2 litres (2 pints) vegetable stock

150 ml ($^1/_4$ pint) single cream

For the croutons

4 slices French bread

175 g (6 oz) ripe Crozier blue cheese, sliced

salt and freshly ground black pepper

Preheat the oven to 200°C/400°F/Gas 6. Place the swede into a roasting tray and drizzle over two tablespoons of the olive oil. Season generously and roast for 35–40 minutes until golden brown and tender, shaking the tin occasionally to ensure even cooking.

Meanwhile, heat the remaining tablespoon of olive oil in a large heavy-based pan and add the onion, carrots, celery, garlic and thyme. Stir well to combine and then fry for 4–5 minutes until softened but not browned, stirring occasionally.

Add the roasted swede to the pan and then pour in the stock. Bring gently to the boil, then reduce the heat, cover and simmer for 25–30 minutes until completely tender, stirring occasionally. Purée the soup in a food processor or with a hand blender until completely smooth. Pass through a sieve for an extra fine texture if preferred.

Preheat the grill. Arrange the French bread on a grill rack and toast until lightly golden on both sides. Cover each with the Crozier blue cheese and return to the grill for a minute or so until just melted.

Meanwhile, transfer the soup to a clean pan and stir in the cream. Gently heat through and season to taste. Divide among warmed bowls and top each one with a Crozier blue crouton to serve.

The entire contents of this soup can be found in a good deli or at a farmers' market. It's great hot or cold and takes minutes to prepare, making it the perfect weekend lunch.

Beetroot soup with horseradish

SERVES 4

450 g (1 lb) cooked beetroot, peeled and
  chopped
1 onion, grated
1 tsp grated horseradish
675 g (1^1/$_2$ lb) thick Greek yoghurt

^{1}/$_2$ tsp celery salt
1 tbsp cider vinegar
^{1}/$_2$ tsp ground black pepper
300 ml (^{1}/$_2$ pint) vegetable stock
salt and freshly ground black pepper
4 spring onions, finely chopped

Place the beetroot in a food processor with the onion, horseradish, yoghurt, celery salt, vinegar and black pepper. Blend until smooth. Use the vegetable stock to thin down the mixture to the desired consistency.

The soup can be served either hot or cold. If preferred hot, warm through in a pan on a low heat, being careful not to allow the soup to boil. Season to taste. To serve, pour into bowls and sprinkle over the spring onions.

This is what I love to eat when I feel a bit under the weather but need my body to keep going. It's a fantastic way of using up a bit of leftover roast chicken and is just the thing for a leisurely lunch or a late-night supper after a big Sunday lunch.

Chicken noodle soup

SERVES 4

225 g (8 oz) fine egg noodles
pinch salt
1 tbsp sunflower oil
1 tsp sesame oil
1 garlic clove, finely chopped
$^1/_2$ tsp freshly grated root ginger
$^1/_2$ tsp finely chopped red chilli
3 spring onions, thinly sliced

1.2 litres (2 pints) chicken stock
2 tbsp light soy sauce
1 tsp clear honey
85 g (3 oz) sugarsnap peas
85 g (3 oz) tiny broccoli florets
175 g (6 oz) cooked chicken, shredded
handful baby spinach leaves
1 tbsp chopped fresh coriander

Plunge the noodles into a pan of boiling salted water for 4 minutes (or according to packet instructions) until tender. Refresh under cold water and drain well.

Heat the sunflower and sesame oils in a large pan. Add the garlic, ginger, chilli and spring onions and cook for 3 minutes, stirring constantly.

Pour the chicken stock into the pan and add the soy sauce with the honey, sugarsnap peas and broccoli. Bring to the boil, then reduce the heat and simmer for 3 minutes until the vegetables are just tender but still retain their colour.

Tip the cooked noodles into the chicken broth and add the chicken with the spinach and coriander. Heat gently for another 2 minutes to warm through, stirring occasionally to combine. Ladle into warmed bowls to serve.

barbecues & picnics

Moveable Feasts

Chilled tomato bisque

Vegetarian Wellington

Chargrilled-vegetable layered sandwich

The Great Outdoors

Sweet and sticky pork ribs

Chargrilled Thai beef salad

Inverted Roquefort cheeseburger with basil ketchup

Butterflied lamb with Moroccan mint mechoui

Sichuan ginger chicken

Nice but not Naughty

Strawberry and mint salsa

Grilled plums with mascarpone

Mango and rum lollies

Serve this in tiny cups or even shot glasses at the start of a barbecue or picnic. It does need to be served good and chilled so use a well-insulated flask to transport it. If you are making this out of season, use a can of chopped tomatoes. Frozen olive-oil cubes are very easy to make: pour extra-virgin olive oil into ice-cube moulds and freeze solid, then use as required.

Chilled tomato bisque

SERVES 4–6

1 small red pepper

1 slice country-style white bread

2 tsp sherry vinegar

1 garlic clove, peeled and finely chopped

1 tsp caster sugar

1 red chilli, seeded and finely diced

2–4 tbsp extra-virgin olive oil

225 g (8 oz) plum tomatoes, peeled, seeded and roughly chopped

2 tsp tomato ketchup

200 ml (7 fl oz) tomato juice

2 spring onions, thinly sliced

$^1/_2$ large cucumber, peeled, seeded and roughly diced

2 tsp ready-made pesto (good quality or home-made)

salt and freshly ground black pepper

frozen olive-oil cubes, to serve

Preheat the grill. Place the red pepper on the grill rack and cook for 10–15 minutes until well charred and blistered, turning regularly. Transfer to a polythene bag and secure with a knot. Leave to cool completely, then peel. Chop the flesh, reserving any juices and discarding the seeds and core.

Cut off the crusts from the bread and discard. Cut the bread up and place in a food processor or liquidizer. With the machine running, add the vinegar, garlic, sugar and chilli and blend until smooth.

Add the extra-virgin olive oil a little at a time to the bread until it will absorb no more. Add the tomatoes, tomato ketchup, tomato juice, spring onions, roasted red pepper, cucumber and pesto, and continue to blend to form a smooth emulsion. Season to taste. Pour into a non-metallic jug and chill for at least 2 hours or overnight.

To serve, season to taste and then ladle the soup into small cups, shot glasses or wide-rimmed bowls. Garnish with the frozen olive-oil cubes.

This dish can be made up to one day in advance and then baked on the day you want to serve it. If you are going to use it as part of a picnic, leave it to cool completely at room temperature before wrapping it in tin foil.

Vegetarian Wellington

SERVES 4–6

375 g (13 oz) packet ready-rolled puff pastry

plain flour, for dusting

100 g (4 oz) risotto rice

450 ml ($^3/_4$ pint) vegetable stock

pinch saffron strands

25 g (1 oz) freshly grated Parmesan

1 egg, beaten

3 tbsp double cream

handful fresh flat-leaf parsley, roughly chopped

handful fresh basil, roughly chopped

200 g (7 oz) jar roasted red peppers, drained and cut into quarters

200 g (7 oz) jar chargrilled aubergines, drained

100 g (4 oz) ball buffalo mozzarella, drained and thinly sliced

200 g (7 oz) jar baby artichokes or hearts, drained and sliced

2 garlic cloves, sliced

salt and freshly ground black pepper

dressed rocket salad, to serve

Preheat the oven to 200°C/400°F/Gas 6. Roll out the pastry on a lightly floured board to 35 cm (14 in) square. Lay the pastry in a 22 cm (8 $^3/_4$ in) × 12 cm (4 $^3/_4$ in) non-stick loaf tin, pressing into the corners and leaving the excess hanging over the sides. Chill in the fridge while you are preparing the filling.

Place the risotto rice in a pan and cover with the stock. Add the saffron, and salt to taste. Leave to cook for 10 minutes, stirring occasionally until the liquid has been absorbed and the rice is nearly cooked. Stir in the Parmesan and remove from the heat; the risotto will continue to swell and cook. Leave to cool completely.

Place the cooled saffron rice in a bowl and combine with the egg and cream, parsley and basil, then season to taste. Spoon half into the bottom of the pastry-lined loaf tin. Arrange a layer of the red pepper quarters on top followed by the aubergine slices, mozzarella, artichokes and garlic. Cover with the remaining saffron rice. Fold over the pastry to enclose the filling, cutting away any excess. Lightly wet your fingers and seal the pastry edges to ensure the filling doesn't seep out during cooking.

Place the vegetarian Wellington on a baking tray and bake for 50 minutes to 1 hour until the pastry is golden brown and all of the filling is heated through. Leave to cool for 5 minutes in the loaf tin, then turn out on to a platter to serve, or on to a wire rack to cool completely. Using a serrated knife, cut into slices and arrange on plates with some salad.

This colourful picnic-style loaf could be made with jars of chargrilled vegetables, but sometimes it's nicer to make your own. If you plan to have a barbecue one day and a picnic the next, make these at the end of the barbecue in preparation for the next day's outing.

Chargrilled-vegetable layered sandwich

SERVES 4–6

225 ml (8 fl oz) olive oil

2 garlic cloves, crushed

4 dried small red chillies

1 tbsp chopped fresh flat-leaf parsley

2 red peppers, cut into quarters and seeds removed

2 yellow peppers, cut into quarters and seeds removed

3 small courgettes, sliced length-ways

2 red onions, sliced into thick rounds (with root intact)

1 aubergine, cut into 1 cm ($^1/_2$ in) rounds

1 rustic round loaf, measuring about 25 cm (10 in) across

4 tbsp tapenade

1 small bunch fresh basil, leaves finely shredded

225 g (8 oz) mozzarella, very thinly sliced

40 g ($1^1/_2$ oz) wild rocket

salt and freshly ground black pepper

Place the olive oil in a shallow non-metallic dish, add the garlic, chilli and parsley, and season to taste. Add the peppers, courgettes and onions. Leave to marinate at room temperature for 1 hour. Toss the aubergines in the marinade at the last minute. Arrange the vegetables on the grill rack over medium-hot coals. Cook for 6–8 minutes until completely softened and richly coloured, turning regularly and basting with any remaining marinade.

Meanwhile, cut a 1 cm ($^1/_2$ in) slice off the top of the loaf. Hollow out the bread with your fingers to leave a case with walls about 1 cm ($^1/_2$ in) thick. Brush the inside with a little of the leftover marinade and spread lightly with two-thirds of the tapenade.

As soon as the vegetables are cooked, remove them from the grill and layer them up inside the loaf, sprinkling each layer with basil and seasoning to taste. I would start with the aubergine, then the sliced mozzarella, the red peppers, yellow peppers, onions (remembering to trim off any remaining root) and courgettes. Spread over the remaining tapenade and cover with the rocket, pressing it down gently.

Replace the top of the loaf and wrap the whole thing in a sheet of greaseproof paper and then a large sheet of cling film. Place the filled loaf in the fridge overnight between two wooden boards and weigh down – lots of unopened cans will do the trick. Allow the whole thing to come back to room temperature, then unwrap and cut into thick wedges to serve.

Try to source baby back ribs, which you should be able to get from a good pork butcher. As they are from a young animal they are much smaller than normal ones, but still have plenty of meat with a much more succulent flavour.

Sweet and sticky pork ribs

SERVES 4–6

300 ml ($^1/_2$ pint) tomato ketchup
300 ml ($^1/_2$ pint) dark soy sauce
120 g (4 $^1/_2$ oz) clear honey
5 cm (2 in) piece fresh root ginger,
  peeled and finely chopped
4 garlic cloves, finely chopped
5 tbsp Amontillado sherry

1 tsp ground star anise (optional)
1 tbsp kecap manis (sweet soy sauce)
1 tbsp chopped fresh rosemary
1.75–2.25 kg (4–5 lb) pork spare ribs
  (still joined, and baby back, if possible)
2 spring onions, finely chopped
buttered mini corn cobs and crispy potato
  skins, to serve (optional)

Place the tomato ketchup in a large shallow non-metallic dish with the soy sauce, honey, ginger, garlic, sherry, star anise (if using), kecap manis and rosemary, and mix thoroughly to combine. Add the ribs, cover with cling film and chill for up to 24 hours, if time allows.

Place the ribs in a large, deep pan – you may have to cut the ribs in half to get them to fit. Pour over the marinade and then add enough water to cover. Bring to a simmer, then cook over a medium heat for 45 minutes to 1 hour until completely tender. Remove from the heat and transfer to a large shallow non-metallic dish. Allow the ribs to cool in the marinade, then cover with cling film and chill until ready to cook.

If using a charcoal barbecue, light it 30 minutes before you want to start cooking. If using a gas barbecue, light it 10 minutes beforehand. When you want to use the ribs, carefully scoop the fat from the top of the mixture and discard, then allow the mixture to come back up to room temperature. Drain off all the marinade and place in a pan over a medium heat, then reduce down to a sticky coating consistency.

Arrange the ribs on a grill rack over medium-hot coals and cook for about 8 minutes on each side, basting or painting the ribs with the reduced marinade from time to time. To serve, cut into single ribs and arrange on a large platter, then scatter over the spring onions. Have the crispy potato skins and corn cobs on the side or in separate bowls if using, and serve the ribs with plenty of napkins and finger bowls on hand.

a quick & tasty weekend supper

This salad is perfect for eating al fresco, whether you decide to cook it on the barbecue or on a griddle pan so that it can be brought along as part of a picnic while it is marinating.

Chargrilled Thai beef salad

SERVES 4

1 tsp jasmine rice

2 dried small red chillies

500 g (1 lb 2 oz) thick beef fillet

2 tbsp toasted sesame oil

5 tbsp kecap manis (sweet soy sauce)

100 g (4 oz) cherry tomatoes, halved

1 small cucumber, peeled, halved, seeded and cut into 1 cm ($^1/_2$ in) slices

4 red shallots, thinly sliced

1 mild red chilli, seeded and thinly sliced

handful fresh mint leaves

handful fresh coriander leaves

handful fresh basil leaves, torn

4 spring onions, thinly sliced

2 tsp caster sugar

4 tbsp fresh lime juice

3 tbsp Thai fish sauce (nam pla)

100 g (4 oz) mixed green salad leaves

If using a charcoal barbecue, light it 30 minutes before you want to start cooking. If using a gas barbecue, light it 10 minutes beforehand. Alternatively, use a griddle or frying pan.

Heat a dry frying pan, add the rice and chillies and toast until the rice is golden but not burnt. Grind the rice and chillies in a coffee-grinder or pound to a powder in a pestle and mortar and set aside.

If using a griddle or frying pan, place over a high heat until very hot. Cook the steak over medium-hot coals on the barbecue or in the pan for 10–12 minutes until well marked on the outside and rare to medium-rare inside. Place in a non-metallic bowl and leave to rest for 10 minutes, then mix together the sesame oil and kecap manis and brush all over the fillet. Cover with cling film and leave to marinate in a cool place for 2 hours, turning from time to time.

Place the cherry tomatoes, cucumber, shallots, chilli, herbs and spring onions in a large bowl and gently toss together to combine. Cover with cling film and chill until needed. In a screw-topped jar dissolve the sugar in the lime juice and fish sauce. Set aside until needed.

To serve, thinly slice the beef and return to the bowl it has been marinating in. Combine the tomato mixture with the fish sauce dressing and ground chilli rice and toss with the beef. Divide the salad leaves between plates and pile the beef mixture high on top to serve.

These fantastic burgers with all the trimmings make the perfect barbecue meal, particularly when served with French fries. They could also be cooked on a ridged griddle or in a frying pan. Your burgers will only be as good as the mince you use, which should contain at least 20 per cent fat. This adds to the flavour and stops them drying out during cooking.

Inverted Roquefort cheeseburger with basil ketchup

SERVES 4

50 g (2 oz) Roquefort cheese

50 g (2 oz) unsalted butter

1 tbsp snipped fresh chives

1 red onion

3 tbsp olive oil

1 leek, finely chopped

2 garlic cloves, crushed

1 mild red chilli, seeded and finely chopped

200 g (7 oz) can chopped tomatoes

1 tbsp shredded fresh basil

675 g ($1^1/_2$ lb) minced beef

4 burger buns, split in half

2 tbsp mayonnaise

1 little Gem lettuce, separated into leaves

1 pickled cucumber, sliced

2 tomatoes, sliced

salt and freshly ground black pepper

Mash together the Roquefort cheese and butter in a small bowl. Season with pepper and stir in the chives. Shape into a short cylinder, no more than 5 cm (2 in) in length, and wrap in cling film. Chill for at least 1 hour or up to 24 hours to firm up.

Cut the onion in half, then cut one half into thin slices and reserve for garnishing and finely chop the other half. Heat the olive oil in a pan and gently fry the chopped onion and leek for a few minutes until softened but not coloured. Stir in the garlic and chilli, season to taste and cook for another minute. Tip in the tomatoes and allow to bubble gently for 8–10 minutes or until the ketchup is reduced and slightly thickened, stirring occasionally. Remove from the heat, season to taste and stir in the basil.

Divide the beef into four portions, then, using wet hands, shape into patties that are 2.5 cm (1 in) thick. Remove the Roquefort butter from the fridge and cut into four even-sized pieces. Make a deep indentation in the middle of each patty and push in a piece of the Roquefort butter, pushing the beef back around the mixture so that it is well sealed. Chill for at least 1 hour or up to 24 hours until ready to cook.

If using a charcoal barbecue, light it 30 minutes before you want to start

cooking. If using a gas barbecue, light it 10 minutes beforehand. Sprinkle a teaspoon of pepper all over the chilled burgers. Add to the grill rack and cook for 4 minutes on each side for rare, 6 minutes each side for medium and 8–9 minutes for well done. Toast the cut sides of the burger buns on the grill rack and place the bottom halves on warmed plates. Add a smear of mayonnaise followed by the lettuce and pickled cucumber, tomato and onion slices. Top with the burgers, then the top halves of the buns, and serve a good dollop of the basil ketchup to the side.

This is one of my favourite things to do on the barbecue – it is very easy to cook and can be carved in seconds. Get your butcher to do the hard work of cutting out the bone and don't forget to ask him to remove the parchment-like covering on the skin.

Butterflied lamb with Moroccan mint mechoui

SERVES 4

2–2.5 kg (4^1/$_4$–6 lb) leg of lamb, boned and well trimmed, roughly 4–5 cm (1^1/$_2$–2 in) thick

25 g (1 oz) chopped fresh mint, plus extra to garnish

finely grated rind and juice 2 lemons

4 garlic cloves, finely chopped

2 tbsp ground coriander

2 tsp paprika

2 tsp ground cumin

2 tsp coarsely ground black pepper

1 tsp cayenne pepper

4 tbsp extra-virgin olive oil

good pinch of salt

fresh green salad and couscous, to serve (optional)

Place the lamb in a shallow non-metallic dish. Mix together the remaining ingredients, except the salt, and rub over the meat. Cover tightly with plastic film and chill overnight or, if time is short, leave to stand at room temperature for 2–3 hours, turning the lamb over from time to time.

When you are ready to cook, if the lamb has been chilled overnight, bring it back to room temperature. If using a charcoal barbecue, light it 30 minutes before you want to start cooking. If using a gas barbecue, light it 10 minutes beforehand. Cook the lamb over medium-hot coals for about 40 minutes for medium-rare lamb, turning occasionally. Leave to rest in a warm place for 10 minutes. If you don't like your lamb too pink you can cover it with foil at this point and it will continue to cook. Carve into slices, scatter over the mint to garnish and serve at once with the salad and couscous, if liked.

As this chicken cooks, the marinade will blacken in places, but as it falls off it will leave behind a well-flavoured, crisp skin, with lovely moist tender meat beneath.

Sichuan ginger chicken

SERVES 4

1 tbsp Sichuan peppercorns

3 tbsp freshly grated root ginger

4 garlic cloves, finely chopped

finely grated rind of 3 oranges

4 spring onions, finely chopped

1 red chilli, seeded and finely chopped

2 tbsp clear honey

2 tbsp dark soy sauce

150 ml (¹/₄ pint) corn oil

4 tbsp sesame oil

4 part-boned chicken breasts or 12 large
   chicken wings

2 tbsp chopped fresh coriander

salt and freshly ground black pepper

rice salad, to serve (optional)

Place the Sichuan peppercorns in a small frying pan and toast for a few minutes until aromatic, tossing occasionally, then grind to a powder in a mini blender or pestle and mortar. Add the ginger to the ground pepper, with the garlic, orange rind, spring onions and chilli, and blitz or pound to a smooth paste. Transfer to a large plastic container with a lid and add the honey, soy sauce and corn and sesame oils. Season to taste and stir until well combined.

Add the chicken breasts or wings to the Sichuan mixture, turning to coat, then secure the lid and leave to marinate in the fridge for at least 4 hours or preferably overnight, shaking the container occasionally.

When you are ready to cook, if using a charcoal barbecue, light it 30 minutes before you want to start. If using a gas barbecue, light it 10 minutes beforehand. Cook the chicken breasts over medium-hot coals for 25–30 minutes or the wings for 20–25 minutes, basting now and then with the leftover marinade. Arrange on plates, scatter with fresh coriander and serve with some rice salad, if liked.

Strawberry and mint salsa

SERVES 4

1 tbsp balsamic vinegar

1 tbsp fraise (strawberry) liqueur

1 tbsp dark muscovado sugar

450 g (1 lb) strawberries, hulled and cut
 into equal-sized pieces

20 g ($^3/_4$ oz) fresh mint leaves

vanilla ice cream or thick Greek yoghurt,
 to serve

Heat the balsamic vinegar in a pan with the fraise liqueur. Add the sugar and simmer gently until the sugar dissolves, stirring occasionally. Pour into a bowl and leave to cool.

Once the balsamic mixture is at room temperature, tip in the strawberries. Chop 1 tablespoon of the mint, then fold the chopped and whole mint leaves into the mixture. Divide between small bowls and top each one with a scoop of ice cream or a dollop of yoghurt to serve.

Grilled plums with mascarpone

SERVES 4

6 firm ripe plums

2 meringue nests (about 40 g
 ($1^1/_2$ oz) in total)

4–6 tbsp mascarpone cheese

4 tbsp caster sugar

Preheat the oven to 200°C/400°F/Gas 6. Cut the plums in half and remove the stones. Arrange them in a small roasting tin, cut-side up.

Crush the meringues and sprinkle them into the hollows of the plums and add a spoonful of mascarpone on top. Sprinkle with the caster sugar and bake for 20 minutes until the plums are tender with a crisp crust. Bring the dish straight to the table and allow guests to help themselves.

Mango and rum lollies

SERVES 10–12

175 g (6 oz) caster sugar
finely pared rind 4 limes, all white pith
  removed

2 large ripe mangoes, peeled and flesh cut
  away from the stones
4 tbsp white rum
juice 2 limes

Place the sugar in a pan and pour in 175 ml (6 fl oz) of water. Place over a very gentle heat and allow the sugar to dissolve, without boiling, until completely clear. Then bring the syrup to the boil and boil for 4–5 minutes or until it is 102°C/215°F – short thread stage. Remove from the heat and place the pan in a basin filled with cold water to cool the syrup down slightly. Stir in the lime rind and allow to chill. You should have 120 ml (4 fl oz) of the lime sugar syrup in total.

Meanwhile, place the mango in a food processor and process for 1–2 minutes or until the flesh has liquefied. Strain through a sieve into a large jug and stir in the lime sugar syrup, rum and lime juice. Pour the mixture into 10–12 ice-lolly moulds. Place in the freezer for 4–6 hours or until the lollies are completely frozen. Quickly dip the moulds into boiling hot water to remove the lollies and hand around to serve.

dinner parties

Spring Menu

●

*Parma-ham-wrapped
asparagus with
tapenade*

*Rack of lamb with a
pistachio crust*

*Easy springtime
vegetables*

Adult jelly and custard

Summer Menu

●

*Stuffed courgette
flowers*

Paella

*Fresh green salad with
rocket*

*Chocolate parfait with
fresh summer berries*

Autumn Menu

●

Mixed mezze platter

Herb-scented couscous

*Moroccan chicken
tagine*

*Caramelized apples
with Calvados ice
cream*

Winter Menu

●

*Roast beetroot with
citrus dressing*

*Chateaubriand with
Béarnaise sauce*

*Passion fruit
meringues*

This starter celebrates the coming of spring by using the first British asparagus, which is in season for roughly eight weeks in May and June. This recipe uses small, tender specimens to create a simple, light dish.

Parma-ham-wrapped asparagus with tapenade

SERVES 4

20 small asparagus spears, trimmed

20 slices Parma ham

For the Tapenade

225 g (8 oz) pitted black olives, marinated in olive oil and drained

40 g (1¹/₂ oz) capers, drained and rinsed

6 fresh basil leaves, torn

1¹/₂ tsp aged red wine vinegar

1 tsp Dijon mustard

85 ml (3 fl oz) extra-virgin olive oil, plus a little extra

2 tbsp chopped fresh flat-leaf parsley (optional)

salt and freshly ground pepper

To make the tapenade, place the olives, capers and basil in a mini food processor or liquidizer. Add the vinegar, mustard, olive oil, and half a teaspoon of pepper. Blend until smoothish, allowing some texture to remain. Fold in the parsley, if using, and season to taste. Transfer to a bowl and cover with cling film, then chill until ready to use.

Cook the asparagus spears for 3–6 minutes, depending on their size, in a large pan of boiling water or in a steamer standing in 7.5 cm (3 in) boiling water until just tender. Drain and quickly refresh in a bowl of ice-cold water, then set aside until completely cool.

Spread each slice of Parma ham with some of the tapenade and then use to wrap each cooked asparagus spear. Arrange on plates or one large platter. Drizzle over a little extra olive oil and add a light grinding of pepper to serve.

Spring is when British products start to come into their own: wonderful new-season lamb served with the first crop of potatoes, after a first course of asparagus. Foods taste much better when eaten in their true seasons. Ask your butcher to French-trim the racks of lamb for you: to remove the meat and fat from the upper 5–6 cm (2–2½ in) of the ribs, leaving clean bones exposed at the top.

Rack of lamb with a pistachio crust

SERVES 4

2 x 6–7-bone best ends of lamb, each about
    275–350 g (10–12 oz)
about 1 tsp prepared English mustard

For the Pistachio Crust
40 g (1½ oz) unsalted butter
50 g (2 oz) shelled pistachio nuts
2 tsp fresh soft thyme leaves

2 tbsp snipped fresh chives
2 tbsp chopped fresh flat-leaf parsley
50 g (2 oz) fresh white breadcrumbs
finely grated rind of ½ lemon
1 small garlic clove, roughly chopped
salt and freshly ground black pepper
boiled new potatoes and Easy Springtime
    Vegetables, to serve (see opposite)

Preheat the oven to 200°C/400°F/Gas 6. To make the pistachio crust, melt the butter in a small pan or in the microwave. Place in a food processor with the pistachio nuts and herbs and blitz until bright green. Add the breadcrumbs, lemon rind, garlic and seasoning and blend again for just a few seconds until all the ingredients are well combined.

Place the racks of lamb on a chopping board and, using a pastry brush, spread the mustard thickly over the fat side of each rack. Cover with the pistachio crust, using your hands to mould it over the lamb. Arrange the lamb, coated-side up, on a baking sheet and chill for 30 minutes or up to 2 hours to allow the crust to 'set'.

Place the racks of lamb in a small roasting tin and roast for 20–25 minutes, or a little longer if you don't like your lamb too pink. Remove the lamb from the oven and set aside in a warm place to rest for 10–15 minutes, then carve into chops and serve with the boiled new potatoes and vegetables.

If you're lucky enough to be buying fresh podded peas for this recipe, choose ones on the small side that are bright green and plump. If you cannot get really good fresh peas, use frozen instead.

Easy springtime vegetables

SERVES 4

3 tbsp olive oil

4 garlic cloves, sliced

6 spring onions, chopped

2 fresh thyme sprigs, leaves only, chopped

300 g (10 oz) jar baby artichoke hearts preserved in oil, drained

350 g (12 oz) fresh podded or frozen peas

1 lemon

knob butter

small handful fresh flat-leaf parsley, chopped

salt and freshly ground black pepper

Heat the olive oil in a large pan, add the garlic and spring onions, then cook over a medium heat for 5 minutes until the spring onions have softened but not coloured. Add the thyme with the artichokes and peas, stirring to combine.

Finely grate the rind from the lemon and reserve, then cut the lemon in half and add a squeeze of the juice to the pan. Cook for 5 minutes until the peas are completely tender. Stir in the reserved lemon rind with the butter and parsley and season to taste. Tip into a warmed bowl to serve.

My wife Jay loves serving this version of jelly and custard.
The custards can be made in advance, with very little to do
at the last minute. They are topped with a burnt butter
sabayon, which can be tricky to make. It is important to
whisk it continuously while it cools, to prevent it splitting.

Adult jelly and custard

SERVES 4

2 oranges

2 gelatine leaves

600 ml (1 pint) Sauternes or orange Muscat wine
    (sweet)

For the Sabayon

150 ml (*¹/₄ pint*) freshly squeezed orange juice

300 ml (*¹/₂ pint*) Sauternes or orange Muscat
    wine (sweet)

3 egg yolks

1*¹/₂* tbsp caster sugar

25 g (1 oz) unsalted butter

150 ml (*¹/₄ pint*) double cream

chopped pistachio nuts and finely pared orange
    rind, to decorate

Using a very sharp knife, remove the skin and white pith from all of the
oranges, then cut into segments. Arrange in the bottom of four Martini
glasses and set aside.

Place the gelatine in a bowl of cold water and set aside for 10 minutes.
Drain and gently squeeze dry. Place in a small pan with a little drop of the
wine and heat gently until dissolved.

Warm the remaining wine in a separate pan and stir in the dissolved
gelatine mixture. Pass through a fine sieve into a jug. Pour over the orange
segments, trying not to disturb the fruit too much. Leave to cool completely
and then chill for 3 hours until softly set.

Once the jellies are softly set, make the sabayon. Reserve three tablespoons of the orange juice and place the remainder in a small pan with the
wine and bring to the boil over a high heat. Reduce the heat and continue
to simmer for 15–20 minutes or until the liquid has reduced to about three
tablespoons. This reduction should be quite thick and syrupy.

Place the egg yolks in a heatproof bowl with the reserved orange juice and
the sugar. Set over a pan of simmering water and whisk for 8–10 minutes
until thick and foamy. Remove from the heat and whisk in the reduced
orange juice and wine mixture.

Heat the butter in a small pan until it is just beginning to brown but not
burn, then quickly whisk into the sabayon. Sit in a bowl of ice and continue
to whisk until the sabayon has cooled completely.

an extra-special 'adult' dessert

In a separate bowl, whisk the cream until ribboning, and then fold into the cooled sabayon. Remove the jellies from the fridge and spoon the sabayon on top. These can be served at once or chilled for up to 24 hours until needed. Decorate with the chopped pistachio nuts and orange rind just before serving.

Home-grown courgette flowers are available from mid-June until October, with imports from Spain, France and Italy coming on sale earlier in the spring. They're always a big treat in our house as we grow them in the garden, but you can get them from good greengrocers.

Stuffed courgette flowers

SERVES 4

8 courgette flowers

100 g (4 oz) ricotta cheese

100 g (4 oz) ball mozzarella cheese, diced

6 tbsp freshly grated Parmesan

handful fresh basil leaves, ripped

good pinch freshly grated nutmeg

light olive oil, for deep-frying

200 g (7 oz) self-raising flour, plus extra for dusting

600 ml (1 pint) sparkling water

For the Pan-fried Cherry Tomatoes

2 tbsp olive oil

1 red onion, thinly sliced

1 garlic clove, finely chopped

1 small dried red chilli

350 g (12 oz) cherry tomatoes

1 tbsp balsamic vinegar

1 tsp chopped fresh oregano

salt and freshly ground black pepper

Gently rinse and dry the courgette flowers, using a pastry brush to remove any dirt. Cut out the stamen from each of the flowers.

Place the ricotta in a bowl with the mozzarella, Parmesan, basil and nutmeg. Season to taste and, with a teaspoon, use to fill the courgette flowers, twisting the end of each flower to keep the stuffing in place.

To cook the tomatoes, gently heat the olive oil in a frying pan. Add the red onion, garlic and chilli and cook for 5–10 minutes until the onion is soft and lightly golden, stirring occasionally. Add the cherry tomatoes and cook for another 3–4 minutes until they begin to soften. Drizzle over the balsamic vinegar and scatter the oregano on top, shaking the pan continuously. Cook for 1 more minute, then season to taste and set aside until needed.

To cook the stuffed courgette flowers, pour enough light olive oil into a high-sided frying pan so that it comes up to a level of 3 cm (1¼ in). Make the batter just before you want to use it. Sift the flour into a large bowl and add a good pinch of salt. Make a well in the centre and quickly pour in the sparkling water, mixing continuously until you have achieved a nearly smooth batter, taking care not to over-mix it. The batter should look lumpy.

Lightly dust the stuffed courgette flowers in the flour and, working in small batches, quickly dip them in the batter, swirling to coat, then carefully lower them into the hot oil. Deep-fry for 1–2 minutes until the batter is crisp and golden. Remove with tongs and drain on kitchen paper.

Arrange the courgette flowers on warmed plates with the pan-fried cherry tomatoes and serve at once.

This is one-pot dining at its best, and looks very special cooked in a traditional paellera. We brought one home from Spain many, many years ago and it's still in perfect condition. I prepare paella slightly differently from the traditional method in that I cook some of the shellfish separately to prevent it from becoming tough and rubbery.

Paella

SERVES 4

600 ml (1 pint) chicken stock

pinch saffron strands, soaked in a little warm water

about 4 tbsp olive oil

85 g (3 oz) raw chorizo, cut into thin slices

50 g (2 oz) pancetta, cut into small dice

4 skinless, boneless chicken thighs, well trimmed and each cut in half

2 garlic cloves, finely chopped

1 Spanish onion, finely diced

1 small red pepper, seeded and diced

1 tsp fresh soft thyme leaves

good pinch dried red chilli flakes

300 ml (1/2 pint) Spanish short-grain rice (calasparra)

1/2 tsp paprika

4 tbsp dry white wine

50 g (2 oz) fresh or frozen peas

2 large tomatoes, peeled, seeded and diced

100 g (4 oz) small clams, cleaned

1 head garlic, cloves separated but not peeled

12 raw jumbo prawns, shells intact

225 g (8 oz) squid, cleaned and chopped into bite-sized pieces

salt and freshly ground black pepper

fresh flat-leaf parsley sprigs, to garnish

Fresh Green Salad with Rocket, to serve (see opposite)

Heat the stock and saffron in a pan to boiling point. Heat half the olive oil in a paellera (traditional paella dish) or large heavy-based frying pan. Add the chorizo and pancetta and fry for a few minutes until crisp and lightly golden, then transfer to a plate and set aside. Add the chicken pieces to the pan and fry for a few minutes on each side until golden, then remove and set aside with the chorizo and pancetta.

Add half the remaining olive oil to the pan. Add the garlic, onion and pepper and cook for another few minutes until the vegetables have softened but not coloured, stirring occasionally.

Add the thyme to the pan with the chilli flakes and rice and stir for about 2 minutes or until all the grains of rice are nicely coated and glossy. Stir in the paprika, then pour in the wine and allow it to bubble down a little, stirring. Pour in the hot chicken stock, add the cooked chorizo, pancetta and chicken, and cook for about 5 minutes, stirring occasionally.

Fold in the peas and tomatoes and season to taste. Put the clams in the paella, with the edges that will open facing upwards, and continue to cook gently for another 10–15 minutes or until the rice is just tender. Remove from the hob and leave to rest in a warm place for 10 minutes.

Meanwhile, heat the remaining oil in a separate large frying pan. Stir in the unpeeled garlic cloves and then quickly tip in the prawns. Stir-fry for a minute or two, then scatter the prawns over the paella, leaving the garlic cloves behind. Add the squid to the pan and stir-fry for 1 minute or so until just tender, then scatter the squid over the paella; discard the garlic. Garnish with the parsley sprigs and serve immediately, straight from the paellera, with the salad on the side.

Fresh green salad with rocket

SERVES 4

100 g (4 oz) bag mixed green salad leaves
40 g (1¹/₂ oz) rocket leaves
1 tsp balsamic vinegar
1 tsp freshly squeezed lemon juice
3 tbsp extra-virgin olive oil
salt and freshly ground black pepper

Place the green salad leaves in a large bowl with the rocket, tossing to combine. Cover with cling film and chill until needed.

Mix the balsamic vinegar with the lemon juice in a screw-topped jar. Season to taste and shake until the salt has dissolved. Add the olive oil and shake again until emulsified. Chill until needed.

To serve, pour over enough of the dressing to barely coat the leaves, tossing to combine. Divide between plates or serve in the bowl.

There are now a number of good-quality shop-bought raspberry sauces on the market, but if you'd like to make your own simply empty a punnet of raspberries into a food processor or liquidizer, add a squeeze of lemon juice and enough icing sugar to sweeten, and blend to a purée. Pass through a sieve and use as required.

Chocolate parfait with fresh summer berries

SERVES 4

85 g (3 oz) plain chocolate (at least 70 per cent
   cocoa solids)
40 g (1¹/₂ oz) unsalted butter
5 tbsp caster sugar
2 eggs, separated
1 tbsp brandy

3 tbsp cocoa powder
175 g (6 oz) fresh cherries, stoned and chopped
150 ml (¹/₄ pint) double cream
grapeseed oil, for greasing
225 g (8 oz) mixed summer berries, such as
   blueberries, strawberries and raspberries
raspberry sauce, to serve (optional)

Break the chocolate into pieces and melt with half the butter in a heat-proof bowl set over a pan of simmering water. Leave to cool slightly.

Place the rest of the butter in a bowl with two tablespoons of the sugar and, using an electric mixer, beat until light and fluffy, then gradually beat in the egg yolks, brandy and cocoa powder – adding a little cocoa after each addition of egg yolk stops the mixture from splitting. Fold in the cooled melted chocolate mixture with the chopped cherries.

Place the cream in a bowl and whisk until it forms soft peaks. Whisk the egg whites in a separate bowl until they have also formed soft peaks, then add the remaining sugar and beat until stiff and glossy. Fold the cream into the chocolate mixture and finally fold in the egg whites until just combined.

Line a 450 g (1 lb) loaf tin with oiled cling film and carefully pour in the chocolate mixture. Cover with cling film and freeze for at least 4 hours or preferably overnight until solid.

Remove the parfait from the freezer about 20 minutes before you are ready to serve, then turn out on to a flat plate and carefully peel away the cling film. Cut into slices and arrange on plates with the summer berries and a dribble of raspberry sauce, if liked.

This informal mezze platter looks stunning. The dishes can be prepared in advance and the platter put together in a matter of minutes.

Mixed mezze platter

SERVES 4

2 aubergines

olive oil, for brushing

2 tbsp extra-virgin olive oil

5 tbsp thick Greek yoghurt

2 tbsp tahini (sesame seed paste)

1 tbsp fresh lemon juice

1 garlic clove, crushed

2 tbsp chopped fresh coriander

For the Mediterranean Carrots

225 g (8 oz) carrots, sliced on the diagonal into chunks

2 tbsp olive oil

$1/2$ tsp chilli flakes

2 garlic cloves, finely chopped

2 spring onions, finely minced

1 tsp ground cumin

1 tbsp pine nuts

1 tbsp raisins

1 tbsp chopped fresh coriander

For the Artichoke Dip

300 g (10 oz) jar marinated artichoke hearts in oil, well drained

2 tbsp chopped fresh flat-leaf parsley

100 g (4 oz) feta cheese, roughly chopped

1 tbsp fresh lemon juice

3 tbsp extra-virgin olive oil

salt and freshly ground black pepper

crispy flat bread, to serve

Cut the aubergines lengthways into 5 mm ($1/4$ in) slices and sprinkle with salt. Set aside in a single layer for 30 minutes to 1 hour to allow the bitter juices to be drawn out. This process also stops them absorbing too much oil.

Heat a griddle pan until smoking hot. Brush each slice of aubergine with olive oil and arrange on the griddle pan. Cook in batches for 2–3 minutes on each side until tender and well marked. Arrange on a plate and cover with cling film until needed.

To make the dressing, place the extra-virgin olive oil in a small bowl with the yoghurt, tahini, lemon juice, garlic and coriander. Season to taste and whisk until well combined. Cover with cling film and chill until needed.

To make the Mediterranean carrots, cook the carrots in a pan of boiling salted water for 6–8 minutes or until tender. Drain well. Heat the olive oil in a frying pan and cook the chilli, garlic, spring onions and cumin for 1–2 minutes to soften without colouring. Tip the cooked carrots into the pan with the pine nuts and raisins and cook for 2–3 minutes until heated through, tossing occasionally. Scatter over the coriander and season to taste. Tip into a bowl and allow to cool completely, before covering with cling film until needed.

To make the artichoke dip, place the drained artichoke hearts in a food

processor with the parsley, feta and lemon juice. Blitz to form a smooth
paste and then, with the motor running, slowly add the extra-virgin olive
oil until well combined. Season to taste and spoon into a serving bowl.
Cover with cling film and chill until needed.

To serve, arrange the grilled aubergine slices on one end of a large
platter and season with pepper, then drizzle over the yoghurt dressing.
Pile the Mediterranean carrots in the middle and set the bowl of artichoke
dip at the other end of the platter. Pile up pieces of crispy flat bread
alongside to serve.

Herb-scented couscous

SERVES 4
225 g (8oz) couscous
4 tbsp extra-virgin olive oil
juice 1 lemon

225 ml (8 fl oz) fresh chicken or vegetable stock
(from a carton is fine)
4 tbsp chopped fresh flat-leaf parsley and mint
salt and freshly ground black pepper

Place the couscous in a large bowl and add the oil and lemon juice. Mix well, ensuring that all the grains are coated. Heat the stock in a small pan and season generously. Pour over the couscous, stir well, cover and leave to stand for 5 minutes before gently separating the grains with a fork. The couscous can be left like this for up to 4 hours.

When ready to serve, season the couscous to taste and place in a pan to reheat for a couple of minutes, stirring continuously with a fork. Stir in the herbs just before serving, and serve hot.

This in my opinion is the perfect dinner party dish. It can be made well in advance and improves with keeping. I often start to make it two days before I'm going to serve it. Use chicken thighs for a more succulent flavour; a mixture of thigh and breast also works well.

Moroccan chicken tagine

SERVES 4

2 tsp ground ginger

1 tsp ground black pepper

1 tbsp ground cinnamon

1¹/₂ tsp ground turmeric

2 tsp paprika

¹/₂ tsp cayenne pepper

450 g (1 lb) boneless and skinless chicken pieces, cut into chunks

2 tbsp olive oil

1 large onion, grated

2 garlic cloves, crushed

100 g (4 oz) ready-to-eat dates, cut in half

25 g (1 oz) flaked almonds

1 tsp clear honey

¹/₂ tsp saffron strands, soaked in a little warm water

300 ml (¹/₂ pint) fresh chicken stock (from a carton is fine)

400 g (14 oz) can chopped tomatoes

2 tbsp chopped mixed fresh coriander and flat-leaf parsley

Herb-scented Couscous, to serve (see opposite)

Greek-style yoghurt and fresh coriander leaves, to garnish

Preheat the oven to 150°C/300°F/Gas 2. Place the ginger, black pepper, cinnamon, turmeric, paprika and cayenne in a small bowl and mix to combine, then tip half into a large bowl. Add the chicken pieces and toss until evenly coated. Cover with cling film and chill overnight if time allows.

Heat a large casserole dish and add half of the olive oil. Tip in the chicken and cook over a fairly high heat until evenly browned, then tip on to a plate. Add the remaining olive oil to the casserole and stir in the remaining spices and the onion, then cook for 6–8 minutes, stirring occasionally. Stir in the garlic and continue to cook for 2–3 minutes or until the onion is softened but not browned, stirring constantly.

Return the browned chicken pieces to the casserole with the dates, almonds, honey, saffron mixture, chicken stock and chopped tomatoes. Bring to the boil, then transfer to the oven and cook for 1 hour until the chicken is completely tender but still holding its shape and the sauce has thickened. To serve, transfer the chicken to a tagine or large dish and sprinkle over the coriander and parsley. Serve hot with the herb-scented couscous and garnish with the yoghurt and coriander leaves.

Few taste sensations are as good as biting into your first locally grown apple of the season. Most supermarkets sell the older English varieties in season.

Caramelized apples with Calvados ice cream

SERVES 4

7 egg yolks

175 g (6 oz) caster sugar

pinch salt

600 ml (1 pint) whipping cream

1 vanilla pod, split in half and seeds scraped out

$^1/_2$ cinnamon stick

3 tbsp Calvados

For the Caramelized Apples

4 dessert apples, such as Egremont Russet or Cox's Orange Pippin

50 g (2 oz) unsalted butter

4 tbsp caster sugar

2 tbsp Calvados

Using a balloon whisk or electric hand mixer, beat together the egg yolks, sugar and salt in a bowl until pale and frothy.

Place the cream in a pan with the vanilla seeds and cinnamon stick and simmer gently for 10 minutes over a low heat, stirring occasionally. Remove the cinnamon stick and discard.

Pour the infused cream on to the egg yolk mixture, whisking to combine. Return to a clean pan and cook for 8–10 minutes over a low heat until the custard coats the back of a wooden spoon, stirring continuously. Pour the custard into a bowl and allow to cool, stirring occasionally. Cover with cling film and chill for at least 1 hour or up to 24 hours.

Stir the Calvados into the custard, pour into an ice-cream machine and freeze according to manufacturer's instructions. Alternatively you can freeze it in a rigid plastic container with a lid, and stir it every half an hour or so to prevent large ice crystals forming.

Remove the ice cream from the freezer and leave at room temperature to soften. Heat a large frying pan. Peel, core and cut each apple into eight wedges. Add the butter to the pan and once foaming, tip in the apples. Sprinkle the sugar over the apples and cook over a fairly high heat for about 10 minutes until the apples are tender and a rich golden brown, tossing regularly. Stir in the Calvados and warm through. Divide between warmed plates and add a couple of scoops of Calvados ice cream to each one to serve.

Beetroot is underappreciated as a vegetable in this country and lots of people are put off at the thought of preparing it. Roasting beetroot in its skin takes away much of the work and also stops your hands getting stained. This is a wonderfully light winter salad that won't fill anyone up before their sophisticated steak and chips main course.

Roast beetroot with citrus dressing

SERVES 4

6 raw beetroot, scrubbed
2 garlic cloves
few fresh sprigs thyme
2 tbsp olive oil

For the Citrus Dressing

1 large shallot, finely diced
2 tbsp white wine vinegar
1 tbsp fresh lemon juice
1 tbsp freshly squeezed
   orange juice
175 ml (6 fl oz) extra-virgin
   olive oil

1 tbsp chopped fresh chervil
$^1/_4$ tsp finely pared lemon
   rind
$^1/_4$ tsp finely pared orange
   rind
salt and freshly ground
   black pepper

Preheat the oven to 180°C/350°F/Gas 4. Place the beetroot, garlic and thyme in a roasting tin and drizzle over the olive oil, tossing until well coated. Roast for 1½ hours until the beetroots feel completely tender, removing and discarding the garlic and thyme once they start to brown too much.

Meanwhile, make the citrus dressing. Place the shallot in a shallow non-metallic dish with the vinegar, lemon juice, orange juice and a pinch of salt. Mix well to combine and then allow to macerate for 30 minutes. Whisk the extra-virgin olive oil into the dressing and stir in the chervil, lemon and orange rind. Season to taste.

Leave the cooked beetroots until just cool enough to handle, then peel and cut into slices. Add to the citrus dressing, tossing to coat, then leave to cool completely, turning the slices occasionally to allow the dressing to penetrate. Cover with cling film and leave to marinate in the dressing for up to 24 hours in the fridge.

Allow the beetroot with citrus dressing to come back to room temperature and then divide between plates, spooning over any remaining dressing to serve.

Order the thick end of the fillet from your butcher for this dish, and ask for it to be as well hung as possible: from 14 to 21 days is perfect. I like to serve this with a big bowl of chips but if you don't like the idea of deep-frying during a dinner party, serve with roasted potato wedges instead.

Chateaubriand with Béarnaise sauce

SERVES 4

675 g (1¹/₂ lb) thick end of a
  whole fillet (called the
  chateaubriand)
1 tbsp olive oil
¹/₂ tsp Maldon sea salt
¹/₄ tsp freshly ground black
  pepper

For the Béarnaise Sauce
250 g (9 oz) unsalted butter
2 tbsp dry white wine
2 tbsp tarragon vinegar
2 tbsp chopped fresh tarragon
1 shallot, finely chopped
¹/₂ tsp ground white pepper
2 egg yolks

¹/₂ lemon, pips removed
1 tbsp chopped fresh flat-leaf
  parsley
pinch cayenne pepper
pinch salt
fresh watercress sprigs, to garnish

Preheat the oven to 240°C/475°F/Gas 9. Allow the chateaubriand to come to room temperature before cooking. Rub all over with the olive oil, then sprinkle with the sea salt and black pepper.

Heat a heavy-based ovenproof frying pan. Seal the chateaubriand over a high heat until golden brown on all sides. Transfer the pan to the oven and roast the steak for about 12 minutes for medium-rare, or to your liking. Remove from the oven and allow to rest in a warm place for 10 minutes.

Meanwhile, prepare the Béarnaise sauce. Melt the butter in a small pan or in the microwave. Combine the white wine, vinegar, one tablespoon of the tarragon, the shallot and pepper in a pan. Bring to a simmer and reduce until about one tablespoon of liquid remains. Strain into a liquidizer or mini blender, pushing down the tarragon leaves to extract the liquid. Add one tablespoon of warm water to the liquidizer together with the egg yolks and turn on. Pour the hot butter very slowly on to the egg yolks. As the sauce emulsifies, increase the butter flow to a thin steady stream.

As the Béarnaise sauce thickens, you will notice a change in the sound of the machine. If the sauce is too thick, add a little more warm water or lemon juice to taste. Add the remaining tarragon leaves, the parsley and cayenne pepper and blend briefly. Season with salt. Keep warm in a bowl or jug set in a pan of hot but not boiling water.

Carve the steak into 12 slices, divide between warmed plates, garnish with watercress and serve with Béarnaise sauce and a big bowl of chips.

Of course you can use shop-bought meringues for this recipe but the result won't be as nice. Home-made meringues keep very happily in an airtight container for up to one week, leaving very little for you to do on the day.

Passion fruit meringues

2 egg whites
100 g (4 oz) caster sugar
4 passion fruit

150 ml ($^1/_4$ pint) double cream
1$^1/_2$ tsp sifted icing sugar
1 pomegranate

Preheat the oven to 100°C/200°F/Gas low. Whisk the egg whites in a bowl until stiff. Whisk in 25 g (1 oz) of the caster sugar, keeping the mixture stiff, then fold in the remaining caster sugar. Spoon the meringue into a piping bag fitted with a 1 cm ($^1/_2$ in) plain nozzle and pipe 16 ovals onto a large baking sheet lined with parchment paper. Bake for about 2 hours or until the meringues are well dried out and an even, pale golden colour. Transfer to wire racks and leave to cool completely.

Cut three of the passion fruit in half and scoop out the pulp. Pass through a sieve set over a bowl, pressing down hard on the seeds to get as much juice as possible. Discard the seeds. Whip the cream in a bowl until soft peaks form and then fold in the passion fruit juice and icing sugar. Cover with cling film and chill until needed.

Cut the pomegranate in half, use a spoon to scrape out the seeds you have access to, then turn the fruit inside out and carefully extract the rest of the seeds. Pick over the seeds, removing all the white membrane, and set aside.

When ready to serve, sandwich the meringues together with the passion fruit cream and pile high on a plate. Cut the remaining passion fruit in half and scoop out the pulp, then scatter over the pile of meringues with the pomegranate seeds.

family suppers

Exotic Eats

Aromatic chicken and green vegetable stir-fry

Beef fajitas with guacamole

Purple sprouting broccoli pasta with Parma ham

Cauliflower and chickpea balti

Winter Warmers

Great pot-roast shoulder of lamb

Fish pie with prawns

All-in-one oven lamb curry

Cottage pie with a twist

Great for Kids

Potato and spinach pasta with steamed salmon

Toad in the hole with mixed grill

Sausage goulash

Frozen choc-nut banana lollies

Simple but stylish. If you like, use pork fillet or sirloin steak instead of the chicken. Remember that all the different components can be prepared a few hours in advance, ready to be cooked off at the last minute.

Aromatic chicken and green vegetable stir-fry

SERVES 4–6

450 g (1 lb) boneless, skinless chicken pieces

3 tbsp light soy sauce

1^1/$_2$ tbsp cornflour

2 tbsp dark muscovado sugar

1 tsp freshly grated root ginger

2 garlic cloves

^{1}/$_2$ tsp dried chilli flakes

8 spring onions, cut into 1 cm (^{1}/$_2$ in) slices

2 tbsp dry sherry or rice wine

1 tbsp rice wine vinegar

150 ml (^{1}/$_4$ pint) chicken stock

225 g (8 oz) mixed green vegetables, cut into 2.5 cm (1 in) pieces, such as asparagus, sugarsnap peas,

broccoli and Chinese leaves

2 tbsp sunflower oil

1 tbsp chopped fresh coriander

2 tbsp torn fresh basil

salt and freshly ground black pepper

plain boiled rice or noodles, to serve

Cut the chicken into 5 mm (^{1}/$_4$ in) slices. Combine half the soy sauce, half the cornflour and half the sugar in a bowl. Fold in the chicken slices and mix well to coat. Marinate for at least 5 minutes and up to 12 hours covered with cling film in the fridge.

Mix together the ginger, garlic, chilli and spring onions in a bowl and set aside. Place the remaining soy sauce and sugar in a jug with the sherry or rice wine, vinegar and stock, stirring to combine. Set aside.

Bring a large pan of salted water to the boil. Blanch the vegetables until just tender: as a guide, the asparagus for 3 minutes, Chinese leaves and broccoli for 2 minutes and sugarsnap peas for 1 minute.

Heat a wok until smoking. Add half the oil and fry the marinated chicken for 2–3 minutes until well sealed and lightly browned. Tip out on to a warmed plate and keep warm. Add the remaining oil and increase the heat. Add the ginger and garlic mixture and stir-fry for 1 minute, then pour in the soy and stock mixture and bring to a simmer.

Combine the remaining cornflour in a small bowl with a little water to form a paste, then stir into the wok. Cook for 30 seconds or until the sauce becomes glossy and thickens. Season to taste. Return the chicken to the wok with the blanched vegetables, coriander and basil, and heat through. Serve immediately on warmed plates with rice or noodles.

This is a wonderful way to feed the family with everyone
making up their own fajitas. The longer the beef 'sleeps' in
the garlic mixture, the better it tastes, then it just needs to
be slapped on a ridged griddle pan or a barbecue.

Beef fajitas with guacamole

SERVES 4–6

3 garlic cloves, crushed

finely grated rind and juice
  2 lemons

1 1/2 tsp ground cumin

1 tsp ground coriander

1/2 tsp cayenne pepper

2 tbsp olive oil

675 g (1 1/2 lb) beef sirloin

12 small soft flour tortillas

275 g (10 oz) jar wood-roasted

peppers, drained and cut into
  strips

275 g (10 oz) jar wood-roasted
  artichokes, drained and cut
  into quarters

200 g (7 oz) jar chunky tomato
  salsa

150 ml (1/4 pint) soured cream

For the Guacamole

2 large ripe avocados

1/2 tsp ground cumin

1/2 tsp ground coriander

2 plum tomatoes

juice 1 lime

1 tsp Tabasco sauce

1 small red onion, finely
  chopped

2 tbsp chopped fresh coriander

2 tbsp extra-virgin olive oil

salt and freshly ground black
  pepper

Place the garlic in a non-metallic bowl with the lemon rind and juice,
cumin, coriander, cayenne pepper and olive oil. Mix well to combine. Trim
the sirloin of excess fat and gristle, then cut into 1 cm (1/2 in) slices. Add to
the garlic mixture and stir well to coat. Cover with cling film and chill for
at least 3 hours or up to 24 hours.

To make the guacamole, cut the avocados in half and remove the stones,
then scoop out the flesh into a bowl. Roughly mash and add the cumin,
coriander, tomatoes, lime juice, Tabasco, onion, fresh coriander and extra-
virgin olive oil. Mix well to combine and then season to taste. Transfer to
a small bowl, cover with cling film and chill until needed.

When ready to serve, heat a griddle pan and a separate frying pan until
very hot. Add the beef slices to the hot griddle pan and cook in batches to
your liking. I cook mine for about 20 seconds on each side until lightly
charred but still medium-rare, but you can cook them for a little longer.

Add a soft flour tortilla to the heated frying pan and cook for 30 seconds
until soft and pliable, turning once. Repeat with the remaining tortillas.

Meanwhile, place the peppers, artichokes, salsa and soured cream in
separate bowls and put directly on the table with the guacamole. Hand
around the platter of beef and soft flour tortillas, allowing each person to
assemble the fajitas themselves.

a tasty treat for the whole family

Purple sprouting broccoli is a wonder that comes into season in March, although because of its popularity many supermarkets are now shipping it in from far away and stocking it all year round. Here I've teamed it up with orecchiette pasta – 'tiny ears' in Italian.

Purple sprouting broccoli pasta with Parma ham

SERVES 4–6

450 g (1 lb) orecchiette pasta
1 tbsp olive oil
175 g (6 oz) Parma ham, thinly sliced
2 garlic cloves, finely chopped
good pinch dried chilli flakes
150 g (5 oz) baby plum tomatoes, quartered

3 anchovy fillets, drained and finely chopped
550 g (1 lb 4 oz) purple sprouting broccoli
50 g (2 oz) butter
4 tbsp chopped fresh flat-leaf parsley
50 g (2 oz) freshly grated pecorino
salt and freshly ground black pepper

Cook the orecchiette pasta in a large pan of boiling salted water for 12–15 minutes or according to packet instructions. Drain well.

Meanwhile, heat the olive oil in a pan with a lid. Add the Parma ham and fry for a few minutes until just beginning to crisp. Stir in the garlic, chilli and tomatoes and fry for another minute or two, tossing the pan occasionally.

Scatter anchovies over the tomato mixture and then tip in the purple sprouting broccoli, tossing to combine. Sprinkle over a tablespoon or two of water, cover and cook for 2–3 minutes until the broccoli is just tender when pierced with a knife, continuing to toss the pan occasionally to ensure everything cooks evenly.

Fold the butter and parsley into the broccoli mixture with the drained pasta. Season to taste and divide between warmed plates. Sprinkle with the pecorino to serve.

The balti sauce can be made well in advance. You could always add diced chicken or tender lamb or beef pieces to the dish (put them in before adding any of the vegetables).

Cauliflower and chickpea balti

SERVES 4–6

2 tbsp sunflower oil

4 onions, chopped

6 garlic cloves, crushed

4 cm (1¹/₂ in) piece fresh root ginger, peeled and grated

4 ripe tomatoes, cut into wedges

1 small cauliflower, cut into florets (about 400 g / 14 oz in total)

400 g (14 oz) can chickpeas, drained and rinsed

1 tsp salt

2–4 mild green chillies, finely chopped

450 g (1 lb) baby spinach leaves

1 tbsp chopped fresh coriander

1 tsp garam masala

For the Balti Sauce

4 tbsp sunflower oil

4 cm (1¹/₂ in) piece fresh root ginger, peeled and grated

2 garlic cloves, crushed

6 onions, chopped

8 ripe tomatoes, chopped

1 tbsp chopped fresh coriander

1 tsp each ground cumin, ground paprika and garam masala

¹/₂ tsp ground turmeric

¹/₂ tsp chilli powder

4 bay leaves

8 cardamom pods, slightly broken open

1 tbsp salt

naan bread or chapattis, to serve

To make the balti sauce, heat the oil in a pan, then add the ginger and garlic. Cook for 20 seconds or so, stirring. Tip in the onions and stir-fry for 5 minutes until they are translucent but not coloured. Pour 500 ml (18 fl oz) water into the pan and bring to the boil. Add the tomatoes, coriander, spices, bay leaves, cardamom pods and salt, stirring well to combine. Reduce to a simmer, then cover and cook over a low heat for 30 minutes until slightly reduced and thickened.

Remove the balti sauce from the heat and leave to cool. Remove the bay leaves and cardamom pods and tip the remainder into a food processor or liquidizer. Blend until smooth. Transfer to a jug and use immediately or cover with cling film and chill until needed.

When ready to serve, heat the oil in a large wok until very hot. Add the onions and stir-fry for 3–4 minutes until lightly browned. Tip in the garlic and ginger and cook for another minute. Add the tomatoes, cauliflower, chickpeas and salt, then fold in the balti sauce until all the vegetables are well coated.

Reduce the heat, cover the wok with a lid and simmer for 5–6 minutes or until the cauliflower is just tender. Fold in the green chillies and spinach and stir-fry for a final 3 minutes until the spinach has wilted. Stir in the coriander and sprinkle on the garam masala. Divide between warmed balti dishes and serve set on plates with naan bread or chapattis on the side.

The meat on a lamb shoulder is the sweetest of all. This is one of our favourite family meals. It also works with a whole chicken: reduce the cooking time to 1 hour.

Great pot-roast shoulder of lamb

SERVES 4–6

1.5–1.75 kg (3–4 lb) shoulder of lamb on the bone
1–2 tbsp olive oil
100 g (4 oz) rindless smoked streaky bacon, chopped
1 large onion, chopped
3 garlic cloves, finely chopped
20 baby new potatoes, scrubbed

2 celery sticks, cut into 2.5 cm (1 in) chunks
2 carrots, cut into 2.5 cm (1 in) chunks
1 tbsp soft fresh thyme leaves
2 bay leaves
400 g (14 oz) can chopped tomatoes
1 tbsp Worcestershire sauce
900 ml ($1^1/_2$ pints) chicken stock

225 g (8 oz) broccoli florets
100 g (4 oz) frozen peas
good handful baby spinach leaves
100 g (4 oz) frozen baby broad beans
salt and freshly ground black pepper

Preheat the oven to 190°C/375°F/Gas 5. Trim the lamb shoulder of any excess surface fat. Add the oil to a large, flameproof casserole with a lid. Over a medium heat, slowly fry the meat on all sides to brown it – this will take 10–15 minutes. Remove from the pan and set aside on a plate.

Add the bacon to the casserole dish and fry for a few minutes, then add the onion, garlic, potatoes, celery, carrots, thyme and bay leaves, stirring to combine. Pour in the chopped tomatoes and add the Worcestershire sauce. Stir well and then pour in the stock.

Return the lamb to the casserole dish and bring to the boil. Put on the lid and cook in the oven for 1½ hours until completely tender. Remove the lamb and set aside on a plate covered with foil, to keep warm.

Add the green vegetables to the casserole and cook on the hob for 6 minutes until just tender. Season to taste. Carve the lamb. Spoon the vegetables and broth into bowls and top with the lamb.

I can still remember the smell of the fish pie as it came out of the oven in all its glory in my childhood. It was a little less luxurious than this version but completely delicious, and has always been one of my favourite things to eat.

Fish pie with prawns

SERVES 6

1 kg (2¼ lb) floury potatoes, such as
   Maris Piper, cut into chunks
100 g (4 oz) unsalted butter
450 ml (¾ pint) milk
150 ml (¼ pint) double cream
2 bay leaves
1 whole clove
pinch freshly grated nutmeg
450 g (1 lb) firm white fish fillets,
   such as halibut, hake or haddock
1 onion, finely chopped

50 g (2 oz) plain flour
4 eggs
1 tsp anchovy essence
2 tbsp chopped fresh flat-leaf parsley
½ tsp soft fresh thyme leaves
1 tsp dry English mustard powder
225 g (8 oz) raw prawns, peeled and veins
   removed
50 g (2 oz) freshly grated Gruyère
25 g (1 oz) freshly grated Parmesan
salt and freshly ground black pepper
fresh green salad, to serve (optional)

Preheat the oven to 200°C/400°F/Gas 6. To make the mashed potatoes, place the potatoes in a pan of boiling salted water, cover and simmer for 15–20 minutes or until completely tender. Drain and return to the pan for a couple of minutes to dry out, shaking the pan occasionally to prevent the potatoes sticking to the bottom. Mash the potatoes, or pass through a potato ricer or vegetable mouli if you like a really smooth finish. Beat in half of the butter and season to taste.

Place the milk in a pan with the cream, bay leaves, clove and nutmeg. Add the fish fillets and poach for 5–6 minutes or until the fish is just tender. Transfer to a plate with a fish slice and set aside until cool enough to handle, then flake the flesh, discarding the skin and any bones. Set aside. Strain the poaching liquid and set aside.

Melt the remaining butter in a large non-stick pan. Add the onion and cook for 6–8 minutes until the onion has softened but not coloured, stirring occasionally. Stir in the flour and cook for 2 minutes, stirring continuously. Pour in the reserved poaching liquid, a little at a time, whisking continuously after each addition. Once all the liquid has been added, reduce the heat and simmer gently for 10 minutes, stirring occasionally until slightly reduced and thickened.

Meanwhile, place the eggs in a small pan and just cover with boiling water, then cook for 10 minutes. Drain and rinse under cold running water, then remove the shells and chop up the hard-boiled eggs. Stir into the white sauce with the anchovy essence, parsley, thyme and mustard powder. Fold in the reserved flaked fish, then season to taste. Remove from the heat and leave to cool, then fold in the raw prawns.

Spoon the fish mixture into an ovenproof dish with a capacity of at least 2.25 litres (4 pints). Allow a light skin to form, then carefully spread over the mashed potatoes to cover. Smooth over with a palette knife and fluff up with a fork. Mix together the Gruyère and Parmesan and sprinkle over the top, then bake for 30–35 minutes or until the pie is bubbling and golden. Serve at once with a big bowl of salad, if liked.

This mild curry is an excellent dish to serve to the whole family or a crowd of hungry teenagers. As everything is cooked together there's the added bonus of very little washing-up to do afterwards.

All-in-one oven lamb curry

SERVES 4–6

550 g (1¹/₄ lb) lamb neck fillets, well trimmed and cut into bite-sized pieces

4 tsp medium curry powder

2 tbsp olive oil

1 large onion, thinly sliced

500 ml (16 fl oz) hot vegetable stock

400 g (14 oz) can chopped tomatoes

2 cinnamon sticks

4 garlic cloves, crushed

4 dried curry leaves or 2 bay leaves

300 g (11 oz) orzo or risoni pasta

1 small butternut squash, peeled, seeded and cut into cubes (about 350 g / 12 oz)

200 g (7 oz) green peas

salt and freshly ground black pepper

strained Greek yoghurt, to garnish

warm naan bread, to serve

Preheat the oven to 180°C/350°F/Gas 4. Heat a large frying pan. Toss the lamb in the curry powder. Add half of the oil to the heated frying pan and fry the lamb, in batches, for 5 minutes until well sealed and lightly golden, tossing the pan occasionally to ensure even cooking. Tip on to a plate and set aside.

Add the remaining oil to the pan with the onion, then cook for 5 minutes until softened and just beginning to colour around the edges, stirring occasionally. Transfer to a 2.75 litre (5 pint) ovenproof dish with the lamb and any juices. Stir in the stock, tomatoes, cinnamon, garlic, curry or bay leaves and season to taste. Cover tightly with foil and bake for 20 minutes.

Remove the foil from the dish and stir in the pasta and butternut squash. Bake for another 10 minutes, then stir in the peas and cook for a final 10 minutes until most of the liquid has been absorbed and the butternut squash is tender. Give it a good stir and season to taste, then divide among warmed plates and add a dollop of Greek yoghurt to each one. Serve at once with the naan bread.

This is my mainstay mince recipe, which I use to make spaghetti Bolognese, lasagne and moussaka. When I go to the trouble of preparing it I'll always make a really large pot so that I can freeze it in small batches to use when the need arises.

Cottage pie with a twist

SERVES 4–6

about 150 ml (¹/₄ pint) olive oil

50 g (2 oz) rindless streaky
  bacon, diced

1 small onion, finely diced

1 celery stick, finely diced

1 carrot, finely diced

2 garlic cloves, crushed

¹/₂ tsp soft fresh thyme leaves

1 bay leaf

¹/₂ tsp dried oregano

200 g (7 oz) can chopped tomatoes

1 tbsp tomato purée

1 tsp anchovy essence

1¹/₂ tsp Worcestershire sauce

450 g (1 lb) minced beef (coarsely
  ground, if possible)

50 g (2 oz) fresh chicken livers,
  finely chopped

300 ml (¹/₂ pint) dry red wine

600 ml (1 pint) fresh chicken,
  beef or lamb stock (from a
  carton is fine)

For the Topping

1 cauliflower, cut into florets

2 eggs

2 tbsp double cream

85 g (3 oz) Gruyère cheese, grated

salt and ground black pepper

Heat a large, heavy-based pan. Add two tablespoons of the oil and tip in the bacon. Cook for a couple of minutes until it is crispy and has released some natural fats, then add the onion, celery, carrot, garlic, thyme, bay leaf and oregano and cook over a medium heat until the vegetables have softened and taken on a little colour, stirring occasionally. Add the canned tomatoes, tomato purée, anchovy essence and Worcestershire sauce. Stir to combine and season to taste.

Meanwhile, heat a large frying pan. Add a little of the olive oil and fry the minced beef in small batches until browned. While the meat is frying, break up any lumps with the back of a wooden spoon. Repeat until all the beef is browned. Drain off any fat and stir the meat into the tomato mixture.

Wipe out the pan with some kitchen roll and add a little more oil, then fry the chicken livers until sizzling and lightly browned. Tip into the minced beef and tomato mixture, then deglaze the frying pan with some of the red wine, scraping any sediment from the bottom with a wooden spoon. Pour this wine, along with the rest of the wine and the stock, into the minced beef mixture, stirring to combine.

Bring to the boil, then reduce the heat and simmer, stirring from time to time, for about 2 hours or up to 4 hours until the beef is completely tender. Season to taste. If the liquid reduces too much, top up with a little water. If time allows, leave to cool, then chill until the fat solidifies on the top. Carefully remove it and discard.

To make the cottage pie, preheat the oven to 200°C/400°F/Gas 6. Place the cauliflower florets in a pan of boiling salted water and cook for 6–8 minutes until tender but not mushy. Drain and place in a food processor. Add the eggs and cream and blend to a rough purée that retains a bit of texture.

Spoon the mince into the bottom of an ovenproof dish and spread the cauliflower purée on top. Scatter over the Gruyère and bake for 25–30 minutes until bubbling and golden. Place directly on the table and allow everyone to help themselves.

Potato and spinach pasta with steamed salmon

SERVES 4–6

4 tbsp olive oil, plus a little extra

1 onion, finely chopped

2 garlic cloves, finely chopped

1 mild red chilli, seeded and finely chopped

1 tsp soft fresh thyme leaves

350 g (12 oz) waxy potatoes, cut into small dice

1.25 litres (2^1/$_4$ pints) vegetable stock

200 g (7 oz) small pasta shapes (ditali, macaroni or penne)

4–6 x 150 g (5 oz) skinless salmon fillets, any bones removed

350 g (12 oz) baby spinach leaves

15 g (^{1}/$_2$ oz) bunch fresh flat-leaf parsley, leaves picked and

sprigs reserved for garnish

85 g (3 oz) freshly grated Parmesan

50 g (2 oz) butter

salt and freshly ground black pepper

lemon wedges, to garnish

Heat the olive oil in the base of a steamer pan. Add the onion, garlic, chilli and thyme. Cook over a low heat for about 5 minutes until the onion is softened but not browned.

Add the potatoes to the onion mixture and stir to combine, then allow to cook for another 3–4 minutes, stirring occasionally. Season to taste. Increase the heat, add the stock and continue to cook for another 5 minutes or until the potatoes are nearly done.

Stir the pasta into the potato mixture. Arrange the salmon fillets on a lightly oiled plate in the top section of the steamer and season to taste. Cover with a lid and cook for 8 minutes or until the salmon is tender.

Turn off the heat and fold the spinach and parsley into the pasta and potato mixture. Leave to sit, still covered, for another 5 minutes.

Remove the top section of the steamer with the salmon and set aside. Fold the Parmesan and butter into the pasta and potatoes. Season to taste and divide between warmed plates. Arrange the salmon fillets on top and garnish with the lemon wedges and parsley sprigs, to serve.

I got this recipe for Yorkshire puddings from Trevor Thompson, a viewer of *Saturday Kitchen*. He has been making them his special way for 60 years; the surprising key to his success is cooking the mixture with cold oil.

Toad in the hole with mixed grill

SERVES 4–6

275 g (10 oz) plain flour
10 eggs, lightly beaten
300 ml (*¹/₂ pint*) milk
3 tbsp olive oil
4 small lamb cutlets
4 Lincolnshire sausages

2 tomatoes, halved
225 g (8 oz) small flat mushrooms, trimmed
1 large onion, thinly sliced
300 g (10 oz) rindless streaky
  bacon, chopped
4 tbsp vegetable oil

For the Onion Gravy

1 tbsp olive oil
2 red onions, sliced
2 fresh thyme sprigs
150 ml (*¹/₄ pint*) red wine
450 ml (*³/₄ pint*) chicken stock
salt and freshly ground black
  pepper

To make the batter, sift the flour and a pinch of salt into a bowl. Make a well in the centre, then pour in the beaten eggs and gradually draw in the flour. Quickly add the milk with 300 ml (¹/₂ pint) of water and whisk until you have achieved a smooth batter. Cover with cling film and chill for 1 hour.

Meanwhile, make the onion gravy. Heat the oil in a pan and cook the onion and thyme over a low heat for about 15–20 minutes until the onion is lightly caramelized. Add the wine and cook for another 5 minutes or so until reduced by half. Stir in the stock and continue to simmer for 10–15 minutes until slightly reduced and thickened. Season to taste, cover with a lid and set aside until needed.

Preheat the oven to 250°C/500°F/Gas 9. To prepare the mixed grill, heat a frying pan until hot, then add one tablespoon of the olive oil and quickly sear the lamb cutlets for a minute or so on each side until lightly golden. Transfer to a platter. Add the sausages to the pan and cook for 2–3 minutes until lightly golden. Pile alongside the lamb chops. Add the tomato halves to the pan and cook for 3–4 minutes until lightly charred and just beginning to soften, then transfer to the platter with the lamb chops and sausages. Add the mushrooms to the oil left in the pan and cook for 2–3 minutes until tender, turning occasionally. Transfer to the platter.

Heat a separate frying pan. Add the remaining two tablespoons of olive oil and cook the onion and bacon for about 5 minutes until lightly golden. Pour the vegetable oil into a roasting tin, swirling it around to ensure an even coating. Pour the batter into the pan and scatter the onion and bacon mixture on top. Arrange the lamb cutlets, sausages, tomatoes and mushrooms on top and bake for 25–30 minutes until risen and golden.

Meanwhile, reheat the onion gravy and pour into a warmed gravy boat. Place the mixed-grill toad in the hole directly on the table with the onion gravy and allow everyone to tuck in and help themselves.

Buy good-quality sausages for this recipe – they make all the difference. I like to serve this with rice, but buttered noodles or tagliatelle also work very well.

Sausage goulash

SERVES 4–6

350 g (12 oz) long-grain rice, well rinsed

2 tbsp sunflower oil

450 g (1 lb) pork sausages, cut into 2.5 cm (1 in) pieces

225 g (8 oz) raw chorizo sausages, cut into 2.5 cm (1 in) pieces

knob unsalted butter

1 large onion, chopped

2 garlic cloves, crushed

1 red pepper, seeded and chopped

2 tbsp hot paprika

2 bay leaves

$^1/_2$ tsp dried oregano

2 × 400 g (14 oz) can chopped tomatoes

300 ml ($^1/_2$ pint) chicken or beef stock

150 ml ($^1/_4$ pint) soured cream or thick Greek yoghurt

2 tsp snipped fresh chives

salt and freshly ground black pepper

Place the rice in a pan with 700 ml (1$^1/_4$ pints) of water, add a pinch of salt, cover and simmer for 10–12 minutes, or according to packet instructions, until cooked.

Heat a large frying pan, add half the sunflower oil and fry the pork sausage for 3–4 minutes until lightly browned, then add the chorizo and cook for 1–2 minutes until sizzling. Remove the sausages from the pan and drain on kitchen paper.

Meanwhile, heat another pan and add the remaining sunflower oil and the butter. Add the onion, garlic and red pepper and cook for 3 minutes until the onion has softened. Add the paprika and fry for 1 minute, stirring, then add the bay leaves, oregano, tomatoes and stock, and bring to the boil.

Add the sausages to the pan and simmer, uncovered, for 10 minutes or until the sauce has thickened and reduced slightly. Stir in the soured cream or Greek yoghurt and season to taste. Divide the cooked rice between warmed plates, spoon over the sausage goulash and sprinkle over the chives to serve.

This is such an easy pudding to make and my kids love getting stuck in with the dipping – although I have to keep an eye on them to ensure that most of the chocolate does end up on the bananas ...

Frozen choc-nut banana lollies

SERVES 4–6

4 ripe, but still firm, bananas
225 g (8 oz) dark or milk chocolate, broken
*   into squares*

50 g (2 oz) unsalted butter
150 g (5 oz) toasted nuts, finely chopped
*   (such as macadamia or almonds)*

Peel the bananas, then cut into chunks about 5 cm (2 in) long. Push a cocktail stick into each chunk. Line a large baking sheet with parchment paper and arrange the banana chunks on top. Place in the freezer for 1 hour until firm.

Place the chocolate and butter in a heatproof bowl set over a pan of simmering water and leave for about 5 minutes until melted, then stir well to combine. Spread out the nuts on a large tray or plate.

Remove the bananas from the freezer and dip them into the melted chocolate mixture, making sure that each chunk is completely coated. Quickly roll them in the chopped nuts to cover completely. Place the coated bananas back on the lined baking sheet and return to the freezer for about 30 minutes to harden. Arrange on a platter to serve.

Sunday brunches

Finger Food

Brown shrimp pancakes

Marjoram and mozzarella fritters

Sukiyaki beef rolls

Eggstravaganza

Caramelized onion, Gorgonzola and herb frittata

Creamy scrambled eggs with roasted field mushrooms and crispy bacon

Smoked salmon eggs Benedict with grated bottarga

French toast with ham and Cheddar

Eating with Friends

Warm salad of scallops and black pudding with pea and mint purée

Asparagus tarts

Roast vegetable and goats' cheese terrine

Salade Niçoise

Dried fruit compote with vanilla yoghurt

Bubbly berry cocktail

Bloody Mary

This Spanish tapas makes an excellent brunch dish. To make pancakes, you need to use a good-quality, heavy-based frying pan so that the heat is conducted evenly.

Brown shrimp pancakes

SERVES 4

olive oil, for cooking

85 g (3 oz) spring onions,
   very finely chopped

85 g (3 oz) plain flour

1 tsp baking powder

$^1/_2$ tsp salt

$^1/_2$ tsp freshly ground black pepper

$^1/_2$ tsp sweet paprika

4 tbsp chopped fresh flat-leaf parsley

225 g (8 oz) peeled brown shrimps

soured cream, to serve

Heat one tablespoon of olive oil in a small pan over a low heat. Add the spring onions, cover and cook for 3 minutes until softened but not browned. Remove from the heat and leave to cool.

Sieve the flour into a bowl with the baking powder and salt. Stir in the pepper, paprika, parsley and cooled spring onions. Make a well in the centre and quickly pour in enough cold water to make a smooth batter,

the consistency of double cream –150 ml ($^1/_4$ pint) should be about right. Fold in the shrimps and cover with cling film, then chill for at least 1 hour, or up to 2 hours.

Heat enough olive oil to come 0.5 cm ($^1/_4$ in) up the sides of a large heavy-based frying pan over a medium heat. Drop in one tablespoon of the batter at a time and allow it to spread out to a pancake roughly 2.5 cm (1 in) in diameter. Cook for 2 minutes until small bubbles appear on the surface. Turn over and cook for another 2 minutes until lightly golden.

Drain the cooked pancakes briefly on kitchen paper, then stack on a plate and keep warm. Repeat until all of the batter has been used up: you should end up with about sixteen pancakes. Arrange the pancakes on warmed plates with dollops of soured cream to serve.

These are moreish and you'll find that they disappear in minutes. Good quality mozzarella makes all the difference. Cook the fritters straight from the fridge for the best results.

Marjoram and mozzarella fritters

SERVES 4

4 x 150 g (5 oz) balls cows'-milk mozzarella, drained and finely chopped
225 g (8 oz) freshly grated Parmesan
2 eggs
4 tbsp plain flour
2 tbsp chopped fresh marjoram
2 garlic cloves, finely chopped
1 mild red chilli, seeded and finely chopped
olive oil, for cooking

For the Spicy Tomato Sauce
2 tbsp olive oil
1 red onion, finely chopped
1 garlic clove, crushed
400 g (14 oz) can chopped tomatoes
1 tbsp tomato purée
1 tbsp chopped mixed fresh herbs, such as flat-leaf parsley, basil and thyme
$^1/_2$–1 mild red chilli, seeded and finely chopped
salt and freshly ground black pepper
fresh herb sprigs, to garnish, such as flat-leaf parsley, basil, chives and rocket

Place the mozzarella in a bowl with the Parmesan, eggs, flour, marjoram, garlic and chilli. Season to taste and gently fold the ingredients together. Shape the mixture into twenty-eight 2.5 cm (1 in) balls and arrange on a plate. Chill for at least 2 hours or up to 24 hours, covered with cling film in the fridge.

To make the spicy tomato sauce, heat the oil in a small pan. Add the red onion and garlic and cook for a few minutes until softened but not coloured. Add the tomatoes, tomato purée and herbs, and chilli to taste. Season generously and simmer gently for 10–15 minutes until the sauce is reduced and thickened, stirring occasionally. Transfer to a bowl and allow to cool. Cover with cling film and chill until needed.

Heat at least 5 cm (2 in) olive oil in a large pan or deep-fat fryer to 190°C/ 375°F. Add a few mozzarella balls and deep-fry in batches for 2–3 minutes until golden. Drain on kitchen paper. Garnish warmed plates with the herb sprigs, add the mozzarella fritters and serve with a bowl of the spicy tomato sauce so that everyone can help themselves.

This is my variation on a classic Japanese recipe, a perfect brunch dish. It is traditional to serve it with a sauce bowl of beaten egg for each person to dip their beef rolls in, but you could offer a sweet chilli sauce instead.

Sukiyaki beef rolls

SERVES 4

450 g (1 lb) beef fillet (in one even-sized piece)

175 ml (6 fl oz) soy sauce

$^{1}/_{2}$ tsp freshly grated root ginger

6 tbsp mirin (Japanese rice wine)

about 1 tbsp wasabi (Japanese horseradish)

2 sheets nori (dried seaweed), 20 x 19 cm (8 x 7$^{1}/_{2}$ in), cut

into 16 strips of 10 x 4.5 cm (4 x 1$^{3}/_{4}$ in)

4 spring onions, cut on the diagonal into thin slices

8 shitake mushrooms, stalks removed and sliced into thin strips

a little cornflour, for dusting

For the Cooking Sauce

2 tsp dashi stock powder

3 tbsp soy sauce

1 bunch spring onions, white parts only cut into 10 cm (4 in) slivers

2 tbsp sugar

25 g (1 oz) cornflour

4 tablespoons sunflower oil

4 beaten eggs, to serve (optional)

Slice the beef fillet across the grain into 16 slices, each about 3 mm ($^{1}/_{8}$ in) thick. Mix together the soy sauce, ginger, mirin and half a teaspoon of the wasabi in a shallow, non-metallic dish. Add the beef slices, cover with cling film and marinate for 1 hour to allow the flavours to penetrate.

Remove a slice of the beef from the marinade and shake off any excess liquid. Place on a flat surface and carefully spread over a little wasabi. Place one nori strip on top, followed by two or three slivers of spring onion and shiitake mushrooms at one end of the beef slice. Starting at the end with the filling, roll up and secure with a wooden cocktail stick.

Place the cornflour on a flat plate and use to lightly dust the beef roll, then place on a platter. Repeat to make the rest of the beef rolls and reserve any remaining marinade.

To make the cooking sauce, place 300 ml ($^{1}/_{2}$ pint) water in a jug with the dashi stock powder, soy sauce, spring onions, sugar and cornflour. Add the reserved marinade and stir to combine. Heat the oil in a large frying pan over a high heat. Add the beef rolls and pan-fry on all sides for 2–3 minutes until lightly browned. Reduce the heat, then pour in the sauce mixture. Simmer the rolls for 8–10 minutes until the sauce becomes glazed and the beef rolls are tender. Remove the beef rolls from the pan and take out the cocktail sticks. Cut each one in half and arrange on plates. Serve warm, with dipping bowls of beaten egg for each guest, if liked.

Originally from Sicily, this frittata deliciously combines the sweetness of caramelized onions and the saltiness of Gorgonzola. Cook it until it is set firm. It is completely addictive: eat a wedge and you'll want more – you have been warned!

Caramelized onion, Gorgonzola and herb frittata

SERVES 4

2 tbsp olive oil
25 g (1 oz) unsalted butter
3 Spanish onions, thinly sliced
1 tsp fresh thyme leaves
3 garlic cloves, crushed
8 large eggs, beaten

25 g (1 oz) freshly grated Parmesan
$^1/_2$ tsp chopped fresh rosemary
1 tbsp chopped fresh flat-leaf parsley
175 g (6 oz) Gorgonzola cheese,
  rind removed
salt and freshly ground black pepper
mixed salad, to serve (optional)

Heat one tablespoon of the oil and the butter in a large sauté or frying pan. Add the onions and start by cooking over a fairly high heat, stirring constantly, until they begin to soften but not brown, then reduce the heat and continue to cook over a medium heat, stirring frequently so the onions do not stick. They will need about 30 minutes in total to caramelize. Stir in the thyme and garlic 5 minutes before the end of cooking time. Tip into a large bowl and leave to cool for at least 5 minutes. Season generously.

Preheat the oven to 180°C/350°F/Gas 4. Add the eggs, Parmesan, rosemary and parsley to the onions and stir well to combine – you should have 1.2 litres (2 pints) of mixture in total. Heat the remaining oil in an ovenproof heavy-based pan about 23 cm (9 in) in diameter and deep enough to take the mixture. Swirl to coat the sides of the pan evenly, then pour in the egg mixture and cook for 2 minutes over a low heat to set the bottom and sides. Break the Gorgonzola cheese into small pieces and scatter on top, then cook gently for another 5 minutes.

Transfer the pan to the oven and cook, uncovered, for about 20 minutes until just set, puffed up and lightly golden. Loosen the sides with a palette knife, cut the frittata into wedges and serve warm or cold, straight from the pan, with a large bowl of mixed salad to hand round separately, if liked.

The knack to this recipe is perfect timing. Some kids prefer their scrambled eggs more chunky. To achieve this, do not whisk the egg and cream mixture – pour or break the eggs straight into the pan and then add the cream, stirring while the mixture is cooking.

Creamy scrambled eggs with roasted field mushrooms and crispy bacon

SERVES 4

8 large-cup field mushrooms, white skin peeled
  and thick stalks removed
$1/2$ tsp chopped fresh soft thyme leaves
2 tbsp olive oil
12 rindless rashers smoked streaky bacon
6 eggs

3 tbsp double cream
$1/2$ tsp Dijon mustard
1 tbsp snipped fresh chives
50 g (2 oz) butter
4 slices multi-grain bread
salt and freshly ground black pepper
fresh long chives, to garnish (optional)

Preheat the oven to 180°C/350°F/Gas 4. Place the field mushrooms in a shallow roasting tin so they fit comfortably and sprinkle over the thyme. Season generously and then drizzle over the olive oil. Roast on the top shelf of the oven for 15–20 minutes, basting from time to time with their juices.

Arrange the bacon on a rack in a separate roasting tin and place on the second shelf in the oven for 10–15 minutes until golden. The bacon will crisp up when you remove it from the oven.

After about 15 minutes, whisk together the eggs, cream, mustard, chives and seasoning in a bowl. Heat half the butter in a non-stick frying pan until foaming. Add the egg mixture and whisk continuously for 2–3 minutes until just set but still soft. Remove from the heat as they will continue to cook.

At the last minute, toast the bread, then remove the roasted field mushrooms and bacon from the oven. Spread each piece of toast with the remaining butter and cut into triangles. Arrange two of the toasted bread triangles on each warmed plate and top each one with a roasted mushroom, spooning over the cooking juices. Spoon the creamy scrambled eggs on top and finish with the crispy bacon. Garnish with the chives, if liked, to serve.

I've garnished this dish with some grated bottarga, which is an increasingly popular form of mullet roe. The roe is soaked in brine, dried in the sun and pressed, then usually wrapped in a coating of beeswax, which has to be removed before eating. Look out for it in specialist food stores or ask your fishmonger about getting hold of some.

Smoked salmon eggs Benedict with grated bottarga

SERVES 4

1 tsp white wine vinegar
4 large eggs
2 soft white muffins
8 slices smoked salmon, about 225 g (8 oz) in total
about 4 tsp finely grated bottarga

For the Hollandaise

1 tbsp white wine vinegar
225 g (8 oz) unsalted butter, diced and chilled
3 egg yolks
salt and freshly ground black pepper

Preheat the grill. To make the hollandaise, place the white wine vinegar in a small pan with a tablespoon of water and heat until reduced to a teaspoon. Leave to cool. Melt the butter in a small pan or in a dish in the microwave and set aside until warm. Beat two tablespoons of water into the egg yolks and then beat into the reduced vinegar mixture. Stir with a whisk over a low heat until smooth and velvety, beating continuously. Add the melted butter, little by little, until you have achieved a thick, smooth sauce. If it becomes too thick, add a tablespoon of warm water. Season to taste and keep warm but not hot or the sauce will split.

Meanwhile, heat a large pan of boiling water with the vinegar. When the water is bubbling, break the eggs in one by one, then move the pan to the edge of the heat and simmer gently for 3 minutes. Remove each poached egg with a slotted spoon and drain on kitchen paper, then quickly trim down any ragged edges.

Cut the muffins in half and place on a grill rack. Toast for 3–4 minutes until lightly golden. Put a piece of muffin on each warmed plate and arrange the smoked salmon slices on top. Cover with a poached egg and spoon over the hollandaise. Garnish with the grated bottarga and serve at once.

Use slightly stale bread for this recipe – it is easier to handle. Experiment with the filling depending on what you fancy: baked beans, Gruyère and crispy bacon work well, as would Parma ham, sliced plum tomatoes and Taleggio cheese with a smear of pesto.

French toast with ham and Cheddar

SERVES 4

4 eggs

225 ml (8 fl oz) milk

4 slices white bread, each about 3 cm (1¹/₄ in) thick

2 tsp Dijon mustard

4 slices cooked ham, trimmed to fit the bread

4 thick slices Cheddar

4 tbsp olive oil

salt and freshly ground black pepper

Preheat the oven to 180°C/350°F/Gas 4. Beat together the eggs and milk with seasoning to taste in a large bowl. Slit open each slice of bread, cutting in from one side, to create a pocket, ensuring that you leave a border of 1 cm (¹/₂ in) around the edges.

Spread the mustard on one side of the inside of each bread pocket and place a slice of ham and cheese inside, trimming them down as necessary to fit. Place the four bread pockets in a shallow dish and pour over the egg mixture. Leave to soak up the liquid for 2 minutes, turning once.

Heat a non-stick frying pan over a medium-high heat. Add half of the olive oil and swirl to coat the base of the pan. Add two of the soaked bread pockets and cook for about 2 minutes until golden brown, then turn over and cook for another 1–2 minutes. Transfer to a baking sheet and then repeat with the remaining oil and bread pockets.

Place the golden bread pockets in the oven and bake for 8–10 minutes until the cheese has melted. Cut each pocket in half and arrange on warmed plates to serve.

Food trends come and go but this is one combination of ingredients that has stood the test of time. Once you've taken your first bite, you'll understand why.

Warm salad of scallops and black pudding with pea and mint purée

SERVES 4

4 tbsp aged sherry vinegar

$2^1/_2$ tbsp sunflower oil

350 g (12 oz) black pudding, peeled and cut into 1 cm ($^1/_2$ in) slices

12 king scallops, trimmed

For the Pea and Mint Purée

50 g (2 oz) unsalted butter

6 spring onions, finely sliced

175 g (6 oz) fresh podded or frozen peas

1 tsp golden caster sugar

300 ml ($^1/_2$ pint) vegetable stock

2 tbsp chopped fresh mint leaves

150 ml ($^1/_4$ pint) double cream

salt and freshly ground black pepper

fresh mint sprigs, to garnish

To make the pea and mint purée, heat a deep-sided frying pan. Add half of the butter and leave to melt until hot and foaming. Tip in the spring onions and cook for a few minutes until softened but not coloured.

Add the peas to the frying pan with the caster sugar, stock and remaining butter, stirring together until combined. Place a circle of parchment paper on top of the mixture and allow to sweat for 4–5 minutes until the peas are completely tender. Remove the paper from the pea mixture, drain any remaining stock and stir in the mint leaves and cream. Cook for another minute or so until the liquid has evaporated. Transfer to a food processor or liquidizer and blend until almost smooth, leaving some texture in the purée. Transfer to a pan, season to taste and keep warm.

To make a sherry vinegar reduction, place the sherry vinegar in a small pan and boil fast until reduced by half. Set aside until needed.

Heat 2 tablespoons of sunflower oil in a heavy-based frying pan. Add the slices of black pudding and gently fry for 1–2 minutes on each side until cooked through and crusty. Remove from the pan and keep warm.

Wipe out the pan, lightly brush with the remaining sunflower oil, then place it over a high heat until very hot. Season the scallops with a little salt, add them to the hot pan and sear for 1–2 minutes on each side, depending on their size, until browned. Remove from the pan.

Place a generous spoonful of the pea and mint purée on each warmed serving plate and arrange the scallops and black pudding slices in overlapping layers on top. Drizzle over the sherry vinegar reduction and garnish with mint sprigs to serve.

These tarts are perfect for a light brunch, especially with a simple tomato salad. A raw fennel, watercress and walnut salad would be a nice alternative, too.

Asparagus tarts

SERVES 4

500 g (1 lb 2 oz) ready-made puff pastry,
  thawed if frozen
a little plain flour, for dusting
unsalted butter, for greasing
3–4 tbsp extra-virgin olive oil

1 large onion, thinly sliced
16 asparagus spears, trimmed
1 egg, beaten
2 tbsp freshly grated Parmesan
salt and freshly ground black pepper
tomato salad, to serve (optional)

Roll out the pastry on a lightly floured board to a 0.5 cm ($^1/_4$ in) thickness. Cut the pastry into four even-sized rectangles, each about 20 × 10 cm (8 × 4 in), and trim down the edges. Arrange on large greased baking sheets, prick all over with a fork and chill for at least 30 minutes.

Meanwhile, preheat the oven to 200°C/400°F/Gas 6. Heat two tablespoons of the olive oil in a frying pan and cook the onion for 3–4 minutes until softened but not coloured, stirring from time to time. Remove from the heat and set aside to cool.

Blanch the asparagus in a pan of boiling water for 1 minute. Drain and refresh quickly under cold running water. Set aside to cool completely.

Spread the softened onion over the pastry bases, leaving a 1 cm ($^1/_2$ in) border around the edges. Arrange the asparagus spears on top to cover the onion completely and brush lightly with the remaining olive oil.

Brush the pastry borders with the beaten egg and sprinkle the Parmesan over the whole tart. Season to taste and bake for 15–20 minutes or until the pastry is puffed up and golden brown. Remove the tarts from the oven, transfer to warmed plates and serve hot or warm with the tomato salad, if liked.

This terrine is full of clean, refreshing flavours and is easy to prepare because it takes advantage of all of the wonderful antipasti now available. It's also a good way to use up the left-overs of a risotto from the night before, in which case there would be very little to do for a spectacular Sunday brunch.

Roast vegetable and goats' cheese terrine

SERVES 6–8

175 g (6 oz) roasted red peppers, drained (preserved in oil from a jar)

1 large bunch fresh basil, leaves picked off and stalks discarded

300 g (10 oz) goats' cheese, thinly sliced into rounds

200 g (7 oz) roasted aubergine slices, drained (preserved in oil from a jar)

250 g (9 oz) artichoke hearts, drained (preserved in oil from a jar)

225 g (8 oz) roasted yellow peppers, drained (preserved in oil from a jar)

For the Risotto

2 tbsp olive oil

1 small onion, finely chopped

1 garlic clove, crushed

100 g (4 oz) arborio (risotto) rice

about 350 ml (12 fl oz) chicken or vegetable stock

100 ml ($^1/_4$ pint) dry white wine

1 tbsp basil pesto (home-made or shop-bought)

juice $^1/_2$ lemon

salt and freshly ground black pepper

dressed green salad, to serve (optional)

To make the risotto, heat the olive oil in a deep-sided frying pan. Add the onion and garlic and cook gently for 4–5 minutes until softened but not coloured, stirring occasionally. Increase the heat, stir in the rice and cook gently for 1 minute, stirring continuously, until the rice is opaque.

Meanwhile, pour the stock into a separate pan and bring to a gentle simmer. Pour the wine into the rice mixture and allow to bubble away, stirring. Add a ladleful of stock and cook gently, stirring, until absorbed. Continue to add the simmering stock a ladleful at a time, stirring frequently. Allow each stock addition to be almost completely absorbed before adding the next ladleful, until the rice is al dente – tender with a slight bite. This should take 15–20 minutes.

Stir the pesto and lemon juice into the risotto and season to taste. Leave to cool completely.

Preheat the oven to 200°C/400°F/Gas 6. Arrange the roasted red peppers in the bottom of a non-stick 550 g (1¼ lb) loaf tin. Cover with half the basil leaves in a single layer, then scatter over half of the goats' cheese and half of the risotto, followed by a layer of the aubergines.

a refreshing, tasty Sunday brunch

Spoon the remaining risotto on top of the aubergines to cover them completely. Slice up the artichoke hearts and scatter in an even layer on top. Add the remaining goats' cheese and cover with the rest of the basil leaves. Finish with a layer of the roasted yellow peppers and press down well. Place on a baking sheet in the oven for 20–25 minutes until heated through, then remove from the oven and leave to rest for 5 minutes before turning out on to a platter. Cut into slices and serve on plates with some dressed salad, if liked.

The tuna for this classic salad is cooked medium rare so that it remains moist, but cook it for a minute or two longer if you prefer, or use canned tuna. The eggs are cooked for six minutes only, so that the yolk holds its shape but is still soft in the centre.

Salade Niçoise

SERVES 4

4 x 100 g (4 oz) fresh tuna
  steaks, each 2.5 cm (1 in) thick
12 new salad potatoes
4 eggs, at room temperature
100 g (4 oz) extra-fine French
  beans, trimmed
4 little Gem lettuce hearts,
  quartered lengthways and
  separated into leaves

4 ripe plum tomatoes, roughly
  chopped
1 small red onion, thinly sliced
6 anchovy fillets, drained and
  cut lengthways into thin strips
16 pitted black olives in brine,
  drained
8 fresh basil leaves, torn

For the Marinade

7 tbsp extra-virgin olive oil
3 tbsp aged red wine vinegar
2 tbsp chopped fresh flat-leaf
  parsley
2 tbsp snipped fresh chives
2 garlic cloves, finely chopped
salt and freshly ground black
  pepper

To make the marinade, place the olive oil, vinegar, parsley, chives, garlic and a teaspoon each of salt and pepper in a bowl and whisk to combine.

Place the tuna in a shallow, non-metallic dish and pour over half of the marinade. Cover with cling film and chill for 1–2 hours to allow the flavours to penetrate the tuna, turning every 30 minutes or so.

Place the potatoes in a pan of boiling salted water, cover and simmer for 15–18 minutes until just tender. Drain and leave to cool completely, then cut lengthways into quarters.

Place the eggs in a small pan and just cover with boiling water, then cook for 6 minutes. Drain and rinse under cold running water, then remove the shells and cut each egg in half. Plunge the French beans in a pan of boiling salted water and blanch for a minute or so, then drain and refresh under cold running water.

Heat a griddle pan for 5 minutes until very hot. Remove the tuna from the marinade, shaking off any excess. Cook the tuna steaks for 2–3 minutes on each side.

Arrange the lettuce leaves on plates or one large platter and add the potatoes, French beans, tomatoes, onion and anchovies. Place the tuna steaks on top and drizzle over the remaining marinade. Decorate with the egg halves, olives and torn basil leaves, and serve.

Dried fruit compote with vanilla yoghurt

SERVES 4

450 g (1 lb) good-quality mixed dried fruits, such as Agen prunes, apple slices, apricots or figs

4 tbsp clear honey

1 tbsp Earl Grey tea leaves or 1 Earl Grey tea bag

$^1/_2$ cinnamon stick

finely grated rind and juice $^1/_2$ lemon

For the Vanilla Yoghurt

1 vanilla pod

1 tsp clear honey

250 g (9 oz) thick Greek yoghurt

Place all the dried fruits in a large non-metallic bowl and cover with 750 ml (1 $^1/_4$ pints) cold water. Cover with cling film and set aside to soak at least overnight, or up to 24 hours is best.

Drain the dried fruits, reserving 600 ml (1 pint) of the soaking liquid, and remove any stones. Pass the soaking liquid through a sieve into a pan and add the honey, then bring to the boil, stirring from time to time. Reduce the heat and simmer for 5 minutes, skimming off any impurities that rise to the surface.

Remove the pan from the heat and stir in the tea leaves or tea bag and cinnamon stick. Set aside to infuse for 10 minutes, then pass through a sieve into a non-metallic bowl or just scoop out the tea bag and cinnamon stick.

Add the soaked fruits to the bowl, along with the lemon rind and juice, stirring to combine. Allow to cool, then cover with cling film and place in the fridge until ready to use.

To make the vanilla yoghurt, split the vanilla pod in half and, using a teaspoon, scrape out the seeds. Place in a bowl and stir in the honey, then fold in the Greek yoghurt until well combined. Cover with cling film and chill until ready to use. This will keep in the fridge for up to 3 days.

To serve, allow the fruit salad to come back to room temperature (or it can also be gently heated and served warm). Ladle into glass or shallow wide-rimmed bowls and add a dollop of the vanilla yoghurt.

Bubbly berry cocktail

SERVES 4

200 g (7 oz) fresh mixed berries, such as
blackberries, raspberries or blueberries

about 2 tbsp kirsch, cherry or blackcurrant
liqueur

$^1/_2$ bottle Champagne, well chilled

Reserve four tablespoons of the berries and place the remainder in a food processor or liquidizer with enough kirsch, cherry or blackcurrant liqueur to taste, then blend to a frothy purée. Pour into a small jug.

Divide the reserved berries among chilled Champagne flutes or long-stemmed glasses. Top with the berry purée, followed by the chilled Champagne. Serve immediately.

Bloody Mary

SERVES 4

400 g (14 oz) can tomato juice
1 tbsp Worcestershire sauce
$^1/_2$ tsp Tabasco sauce
1 tsp celery salt

juice 1 lime
1 tsp grated fresh horseradish (optional)
about 175 g (6 oz) crushed ice
85 ml (3 fl oz) vodka
2 tbsp dry fino sherry

Place the tomato juice in a large cocktail shaker with the Worcestershire sauce, Tabasco, celery salt, lime juice and the grated fresh horseradish, if using. Fill up with ice and shake until very well chilled.

Add the vodka and sherry to the cocktail shaker, then shake again until well combined. Taste and adjust seasoning as necessary. Strain into tall sturdy glasses, top with fresh ice and add swizzle sticks to serve.

Sunday lunches

Spring Menu

Sea bass in lemon salt

Roasted fennel wedges

Warm new potato salad

Rhubarb and ginger Eton mess

Summer Menu

Spicy summer roast chicken

Tabbouleh with a twist

Borlotti and green bean salad

Caramelized raspberry 'pizza'

Autumn Menu

Roast rib of beef on the bone

Yorkshire puddings

Easy green beans

Lemon sponge pudding with blackberries

Winter Menu

Roast loin of pork with apple sauce

Mustard-roasted potatoes and parsnips

Celeriac and mushroom cake

Pear tarte tatin

This is a different way to serve fish. Salt mixed with egg white bakes into a hard crust, trapping the juices of the fish, steaming the flesh and intensifying the flavours. Minimal salt is absorbed by the fish because the skin acts as a barrier. Instead of one large fish, you can make this with four small ones. Reduce the cooking time to 12–15 minutes.

Sea bass in lemon salt

SERVES 4

2 lemons, rind from both, 1 sliced

1 large sea bass, cleaned and scales removed
  (weight 1.75 kg / 4 lb)

handful fresh rosemary sprigs

2 tsp soft fresh thyme leaves, plus 2 sprigs

1 kg (2 lb 4 oz) coarse sea salt, plus extra if needed

1 tsp dried chilli flakes

4 egg whites, lightly beaten

Roasted Fennel Wedges (see opposite), Warm New
  Potato Salad (page 138), lemon wedges and
  melted butter, to serve

Preheat the oven to 220°C/450°F/Gas 7. Chop the lemon rind and set aside. Fill the belly cavity of the fish with the sliced lemon. Remove the leaves from half the rosemary sprigs and set aside. Stuff the remaining whole rosemary sprigs into the belly cavity with the thyme sprigs and season with pepper.

Mix the thyme leaves in a bowl with the reserved chopped rosemary and lemon rind, then stir in the salt, chilli flakes and beaten egg whites. Put a handful of the mixture on to a large baking tray, sit the fish on top then cover with the remainder. The mixture should encase the fish.

Place the crusted sea bass in the oven and bake for 20–25 minutes – the salt casing will turn lightly golden and set hard. Remove from the oven and carefully break away the salt and discard. Transfer the fish to a large dish and serve with the roasted fennel, warm potato salad, lemon wedges and melted butter.

The appearance of fennel is no guide to flavour: perfect-looking specimens can be pale in flavour, while battered-looking fennel can be outstanding. I suspect freshness and the soil it is grown in are the keys. Its flavour is unique among vegetables and is a perfect match for Sea Bass in Lemon Salt (see opposite).

Roasted fennel wedges

SERVES 4
2 large fennel bulbs
2 tbsp olive oil
salt and freshly ground
* black pepper*

Preheat the oven to 180°C/350°F/Gas 4. Trim the hard round stalks at the top of the fennel bulbs and discard the outer layers. Cut the remainder into thin wedges and place in a large, shallow roasting tin. Drizzle over the olive oil and toss to coat, then season to taste.

Place the fennel in the oven and roast for 55 minutes until it has softened and lightly browned, stirring once or twice to ensure even cooking. Transfer to a warmed dish to serve.

It is best to buy new season potatoes in small quantities at frequent intervals. If they are freshly dug, the skins should rub away easily in your fingers. Give them a good scrub; they are well worth the trouble because they look and taste better from being cooked whole.

Warm new potato salad

SERVES 4

675 g (1¹/₂ lb) baby new potatoes
5 tbsp extra-virgin olive oil
1 tbsp Dijon mustard

grated rind and juice ¹/₂ lemon
3 spring onions, thinly sliced
2 tbsp chopped fresh flat-leaf parsley
salt and freshly ground black pepper

Heat a large pan of salted water and, when boiling, cook the potatoes for 10–15 minutes until tender.

Meanwhile, mix together the olive oil, mustard, lemon rind and juice in a serving bowl. Season to taste. Drain the cooked potatoes and tip them straight into the bowl. Sprinkle over the spring onions and parsley and toss through with the dressing. Serve at once.

This is a spring variation on the traditional strawberry dish. The tender pink stems of the first-of-season rhubarb are perfect for this recipe.

Rhubarb and ginger Eton mess

550 g (1¹/₄ lb) rhubarb
85 g (3 oz) golden caster sugar
2 pieces stem ginger in syrup, drained and finely
    chopped

450 ml (³/₄ pint) whipping cream
3 tbsp sifted icing sugar
225 g (8 oz) meringues, broken up into bite-sized
    pieces (shop-bought is fine)

Preheat the oven to 200°C/400°F/Gas 6. Trim the rhubarb and cut into 2.5 cm (1 in) pieces. Tip into a shallow baking dish and sprinkle over the sugar. Cover with foil and roast for 15 minutes. Allow to cool.

Remove the foil from the rhubarb and check that all of the sugar has dissolved. Give it all a good shake, sprinkle over the stem ginger and roast for another 5 minutes until the rhubarb is tender but not mushy, and the juices are syrupy.

Whip the cream and icing sugar in a bowl until soft peaks form. Spoon some of the sweetened cream into the bottom of a serving bowl, scatter over some of the meringues and then spoon the roasted rhubarb and ginger on top. Repeat these layers until the bowl is full, finishing with a layer of cream. Serve immediately.

Marinating the chicken in yoghurt and spices makes the chicken meltingly tender. To test if the chicken is cooked, insert a skewer into the thickest part of the thigh – the juices should run clear. Put back in the oven for another 10 minutes if you need to and test again with a clean skewer.

Spicy summer roast chicken

SERVES 4

1.5 kg (3 lb) chicken

For the marinade

1 whole garlic bulb
a little olive oil
5 tsp caraway seeds
2 tsp cumin seeds
1 tbsp dried oregano

2 tsp dried rosemary
1 tsp turmeric
4 tbsp harissa paste
250 ml (9 fl oz) thick Greek yoghurt
sea salt and freshly ground black pepper
Tabbouleh with a Twist (see opposite) and
    Borlotti and Green Bean Salad (page 142),
    to serve

Preheat the oven to 200°C/400°F/Gas 6. For the marinade, halve the garlic bulb across the middle and place the halves in a small roasting tin. Drizzle the cut sides with a little olive oil and roast for 40 minutes or until golden and the garlic cloves inside are soft and squishy. Leave to cool, then squeeze the garlic out from the skin into a bowl.

Using a food processor or a pestle and mortar, grind the caraway and cumin seeds until fine. Tip into the bowl with the roasted garlic, oregano, rosemary, turmeric, harissa paste and Greek yoghurt. Mix well and season to taste – I tend to use quite a lot of sea salt, but it's up to you.

Rub the marinade over the chicken, both inside and out. Put the chicken in a large food bag, or covered in a non-metallic dish, and leave to marinate for at least 3 hours, or up to 24 hours is best.

Preheat the oven to 180°C/350°F/Gas 4. Cover the chicken loosely with foil and roast for 30 minutes. Remove the foil and return to the oven for another 30 minutes until deep golden and cooked through. Let the chicken rest for 10 minutes before you carve it, then arrange on plates with the tabbouleh and salad.

This is a classic Middle-eastern-inspired salad. It's so good you can serve it on its own – Jay and the kids love it. If you don't fancy bulgar wheat, couscous is a good alternative.

Tabbouleh with a twist

SERVES 4

85 g (3 oz) bulgar wheat
1 lemon
2 tbsp extra-virgin olive oil
50 g (2 oz) toasted flaked almonds
85 g (3 oz) ready-to-eat apricots, chopped
50 g (2 oz) sultanas or raisins

3 spring onions, finely sliced
small bunch fresh flat-leaf parsley, roughly
*   chopped*
small bunch fresh coriander, roughly chopped
handful fresh mint leaves, roughly chopped
3 large ripe tomatoes, seeded and sliced
salt and freshly ground black pepper

Soak the bulgar wheat in cold water for 20 minutes or according to packet instructions, then drain in a sieve and squeeze dry.

Place the bulgar wheat in a large bowl. Grate in the rind of the lemon, then cut in half and squeeze in the juice from one of the halves. Stir in the olive oil and season with salt to taste.

Fold the almonds into the dressed bulgar wheat with the apricots, sultanas or raisins, spring onions, herbs and tomatoes. Season to taste and set aside for 5 minutes to allow the grains to swell – the bulgar will soak up all the liquid. Spoon into a bowl to serve.

This is a super healthy salad. If you want to prepare it in advance, have everything mixed together up to the point where you add the green beans; add the beans just before serving so they don't lose their colour.

Borlotti and green bean salad

SERVES 4

175 g (6 oz) extra-fine green beans, trimmed and cut into 2.5 cm (1 in) lengths

400 g (14 oz) can borlotti beans, rinsed and drained

3 tbsp extra-virgin olive oil

squeeze lemon juice

1 tsp dried oregano

small bunch flat-leaf parsley leaves, roughly chopped

pinch dried chilli flakes

225 g (8 oz) goats' cheese, cut into small cubes

salt and freshly ground black pepper

Bring a large pan of water to the boil and blanch the green beans for 4 minutes until just cooked – they should still have some bite. Drain and refresh under cold running water, then drain again.

Place the borlotti beans in a serving bowl with the olive oil, lemon juice, oregano, parsley, chilli flakes and goats' cheese. Fold in the refreshed green beans and season to taste. Serve at once.

An easy fruity dish the kids will love. It's fantastic made with raspberries in the height of summer, but other fruits, such as apricots, plums, peaches or nectarines, would also be good.

Caramelized raspberry 'pizza'

SERVES 4

plain flour, for dusting

500 g (1 lb 2 oz) packet sweet shortcrust pastry, thawed if frozen

100 g (4 oz) light muscovado sugar

50 g (2 oz) butter

2 tbsp double cream

grated rind 1 small orange

300 g (11 oz) raspberries

For the Raspberry Mascarpone Cream

100 g (4 oz) mascarpone cheese

2 tbsp caster sugar

2 tbsp raspberry cordial or juice

75 ml (2¹/₂ fl oz) double cream

On a lightly floured surface, roll out the pastry to 0.5 cm (¹/₄ in) thickness and cut into four 12 cm (4¹/₂ in) rounds. Lift on to a baking sheet, prick the bases well with a fork and chill for at least 30 minutes or up to 24 hours to allow the pastry to rest.

Preheat the oven to 200°C/400°F/Gas 6. Bake the pastry rounds for 10 minutes until puffed up but not coloured.

Meanwhile, make the mascarpone cream. Soften the mascarpone in a bowl with the sugar and raspberry cordial or juice. In a separate bowl,

whisk the cream to soft peaks and fold into the mascarpone mixture. Cover with cling film and chill until needed.

To make a caramel sauce, heat the sugar, butter and cream together in a frying pan for about 5 minutes or until the sugar has melted into the butter to give a silky, light brown sauce. Remove from the heat and stir in the orange rind.

Remove the pastry circles from the oven and arrange the raspberries in a neat pattern, leaving a 0.5 cm (¹/₄ in) border. Brush the raspberries liberally with the caramel sauce and return to the oven for a further 5–8 minutes until the pastry is golden and the raspberries are still holding their shape. Serve with a spoonful of mascarpone cream in the centre of each pizza (the remainder can be put in a bowl and served separately) and a drizzle more of the caramel sauce.

Roast rib of beef on the bone

SERVES 6–8

1 tsp dried thyme

1 tsp dried basil

$^1/_2$ tsp cayenne pepper

1 tsp sweet paprika

1 tsp garlic salt

$^1/_2$ tsp English mustard powder

2.25 kg (5 lb) piece fore-rib (rib-eye) beef,
  on the bone

2 tbsp Dijon mustard

3 tbsp olive oil

1 onion, roughly chopped

1 carrot, roughly chopped

1 leek, roughly chopped

3 tbsp dripping (from a previous roast)
  or olive oil

150 ml ($^1/_4$ pint) red wine

600 ml (1 pint) fresh beef stock (from a carton
  is fine, or canned beef consommé)

horseradish cream (from a jar), Yorkshire
  Puddings (page 146) and Easy Green Beans
  (page 147), to serve

Place the thyme, basil, cayenne, paprika, garlic salt and mustard powder in a bowl and mix to combine. Wipe the meat with damp kitchen paper and then spread a thin layer of the Dijon mustard all over the fat side of the joint. Sprinkle the spice powder on top, patting it down gently to help it stick. If you have time, wrap loosely in cling film and allow the beef to marinate overnight.

Preheat the oven to 200°C/400°F/Gas 6. Pour the olive oil into a roasting tin and allow to heat in the oven for 5 minutes. Add the onion, carrot and leek, tossing to coat them in the oil. Season to taste and roast for 20 minutes until lightly caramelized.

Increase the oven temperature to 220°C/450°F/Gas 8. Heat a large, heavy-based frying pan, add the dripping or olive oil and, when the oil is hot, quickly sear the beef for about 30 seconds on each side – be careful, as the spices will give off a strong aroma and can make your eyes water. Transfer the beef to the roasting tin, placing it on the bed of vegetables.

Add the red wine to the frying pan and allow to bubble down to burn off the alcohol, then pour into the roasting tin with half the stock. Roast the beef for 15 minutes until well sealed, then reduce the oven temperature to 200°C/400°F/Gas 6 once again and roast for 10 minutes per 450 g (1 lb) for rare, 12 minutes per 450 g (1 lb) for medium-rare, or 20–25 minutes per 450 g (1 lb) for well done. Baste the roast with the red wine and stock every 10 minutes or so during cooking.

Remove the beef from the tin and place on a large dish. Allow to rest in a warm place for at least 10–15 minutes before carving. To make the gravy, pour the remaining stock into the roasting tin and place directly on the

hob to heat. Simmer for 5 minutes, stirring and scraping the bottom with a wooden spoon to release any sediment. Season and pour through a sieve into a gravy boat. Carve the beef into slices and arrange on warmed plates with a dollop of horseradish cream, Yorkshire puddings and the green beans. Hand round the gravy separately.

If you've had problems with your Yorkshire puddings in the past, then try my mate Brian Turner's recipe, which he showed me on *Ready Steady Cook*. The important thing to remember when making Yorkshire puddings is to preheat the beef dripping or oil in the tin before pouring in the batter. The first three ingredients – flour, eggs and milk – are equal in volume, so can be simply measured using a large dariole mould or teacup.

Yorkshire puddings

SERVES 6–8

100 g (4 oz) plain flour
4 eggs, beaten
200 ml (7 fl oz) milk

4 tbsp beef dripping or
sunflower oil
salt and freshly ground
black pepper

Sift the flour and a pinch of salt into a bowl. Make a well in the centre, then pour in the beaten egg and gradually draw in the flour. Add the milk and whisk until you have achieved a smooth batter, the consistency of single cream. Season to taste, cover with cling film and leave to rest for 1 hour, if time allows.

Preheat the oven to 220°C/425°F/Gas 7. Place the dripping or oil into two 12-hole bun trays and heat on the top shelves of the oven for 5 minutes. The fat needs to be very hot to enable the puddings to rise quickly and to stop them sticking to the moulds. Stir the batter, then, using a small ladle, pour the batter into the hot fat so that it comes halfway up the sides. Bake the puddings for about 20 minutes until well risen, crisp and golden brown. Serve at once.

Easy green beans

SERVES 6–8

2 tbsp olive oil

1 onion, finely chopped

450 g (1 lb) green beans, ends trimmed

50 g (2 oz) toasted flaked almonds

2–3 tbsp chopped fresh dill

salt and freshly ground black pepper

Heat the olive oil in a large frying pan, then cook the onion over a low heat for 8–10 minutes until softened but not coloured, stirring from time to time.

Meanwhile, cook the beans in a pan of boiling salted water for 4–5 minutes until softened, but still with a bite. Drain well and tip into the frying pan along with the almonds and dill. Toss well to combine and season to taste. Transfer to a warmed dish to serve.

On baking, this clever pudding separates to form a light, golden sponge over a layer of thick lemon custard. Of course, you could omit the blackberries, but I think they are a lovely ingredient with which to surprise your guests.

Lemon sponge pudding with blackberries

SERVES 6–8

100 g (4 oz) butter, at room temperature,
  plus extra for greasing
175 g (6 oz) caster sugar
finely grated rind and juice 4 lemons

4 eggs, separated
50 g (2 oz) plain flour
200 ml (7 fl oz) milk
100 g (4 oz) blackberries
crème fraiche, to serve

Preheat the oven to 180°C/350°F/Gas 4. Beat together the butter and sugar in a bowl until pale and fluffy. Beat in the lemon rind and juice with the egg yolks, flour and milk – it doesn't matter if the mixture curdles at this stage.

Whisk the egg whites in a separate bowl until soft peaks have formed, then fold into the lemon mixture until evenly incorporated.

Scatter the blackberries on the bottom of a 1.5 litre (2½ pint) buttered pie dish, cover with the lemon mixture and carefully place in a roasting tin half-filled with boiling water. Bake for 30–35 minutes or until well risen and golden brown. Serve straight to the table with a bowl of crème fraiche so that guests can help themselves.

To get a really good crackling, take a tip from the Chinese and pour boiling water just over the rind, leave for about 30 seconds, then repeat a couple more times. Don't be tempted to baste the joint during cooking, and if the rind still hasn't crackled by the time the pork is cooked, remove it as described below and place under a hot grill to crisp up.

Roast loin of pork with apple sauce

SERVES 4–6

1.5 kg (3 lb) pork loin on the bone, skin lightly scored at 0.5 cm ($^1/_4$ in) intervals
2 tbsp cider vinegar
1 tbsp olive oil
2 tbsp coarse sea salt
8 fresh bay leaves
8 garlic cloves, unpeeled
3 fresh sage leaves

1 red onion, cut into wedges
1 glass red wine, about 120 ml (4 fl oz)
600 ml (1 pint) fresh chicken stock (from a carton is fine)

For the Apple Sauce
450 g (1 lb) Bramley cooking apples, peeled, cored and sliced

juice $^1/_2$ lemon
1 tsp caster sugar
25 g (1 oz) unsalted butter, cut into cubes
salt and freshly ground black pepper
Mustard-roasted Potatoes and Parsnips (page 152) and Celeriac and Mushroom Cake (page 153), to serve

Place the pork, skin-side down, on a chopping board and trim any loose fat or connective tissue. Put in a roasting tin, then place in the sink, pour a kettle of boiling water over the pork rind and leave for 30 seconds. Repeat two or three times. Pour over the cider vinegar and massage into the skin to help dry out the rind. Transfer to a plate and leave uncovered in the fridge overnight.

Preheat the oven to 220°C/425°F/Gas 7. Place the pork joint in a roasting tin and drizzle over the olive oil, massaging it into the skin. Sprinkle over the salt and roast for 30 minutes, then reduce the oven temperature to 190°C/375°F/Gas 5. Add the bay leaves, garlic, sage and onion wedges, tossing to coat them in the juices, and continue to cook for 50 minutes or until the pork is completely tender and the crackling is crispy. Nowadays it is perfectly safe to serve pork a little pink.

Meanwhile, make the apple sauce. Place the apples in a pan with 4–5 tablespoons water and the lemon juice. Cook over a low heat for 8–10 minutes until the apples have softened, stirring from time to time. Stir in the sugar and whisk in the cubes of butter, then keep warm. If you'd prefer a cold apple sauce, omit the butter. Spoon into a small bowl to serve.

When cooked, transfer the pork on to a large platter and leave to rest in a warm place for 10–15 minutes. Place the roasting tin directly on the hob and deglaze the pan with the wine, scraping the bottom with a wooden spoon to release any sediment. Pour in the stock, increase the heat and simmer until the liquid has reduced by half. Season to taste, then strain into a gravy boat and skim off any excess fat.

Cut through the fat of the rested joint just underneath the crackling to remove it in one piece, then cut into portions. Carve the pork into slices and arrange on warmed plates with some of the mustard-roasted vegetables and celeriac and mushroom cake, if liked. Pass round the gravy and apple sauce separately to serve.

Sweet parsnips are a hit teamed up with your regular roasties and some hearty mustard. The potatoes can be parboiled in the morning so that everything is ready to go in the oven.

Mustard-roasted potatoes and parsnips

SERVES 4–6

675 g (1¹/₂ lb) potatoes, halved (Maris Piper or King Edward, if possible)

5 tbsp olive oil

2 large parsnips, cut into chunks

2 tbsp wholegrain mustard

salt and freshly ground black pepper

Preheat the oven to 180°C/350°F/Gas 4. Cook the potatoes in a large pan of boiling salted water for 8–10 minutes until just beginning to soften. Drain, then tip back into the pan and give it a good shake until they turn fluffy.

Pour four tablespoons of the olive oil into a large roasting tin and heat in the oven for 5 minutes. Tip in the parboiled potatoes and parsnips, then season to taste. Roast for 50 minutes until just tender and lightly golden, tossing from time to time to ensure even cooking.

Meanwhile, mix together the mustard and remaining tablespoon of olive oil. Remove the cooked potatoes and parsnips from the oven and drizzle over the mustard mixture, then toss until evenly coated. Return to the oven for another 5–10 minutes until the potatoes and parsnips are crisp and golden brown. Tip into a warmed dish and serve at once.

Once prepared, celeriac browns very quickly. If you want to prepare it ahead, keep it in water with a good squeeze of lemon juice.

Celeriac and mushroom cake

2 tbsp olive oil
1 onion, finely chopped
100 g (4 oz) piece smoked bacon, rind removed and cut into small lardons
100 g (4 oz) button mushrooms, thinly sliced

2 celeriac, peeled and coarsely grated (about 675 g / 1¹/₂ lb in total)
2 tbsp chopped fresh flat-leaf parsley, plus extra to garnish
40 g (1¹/₂ oz) butter
salt and freshly ground black pepper

Heat the oil in a frying pan and fry the onion for about 5 minutes until softened but not coloured, stirring from time to time. Add the bacon and mushrooms and continue to fry for 3–4 minutes until the bacon is crisp and the mushrooms are tender. Remove from the heat.

Meanwhile, squeeze the celeriac in a clean tea towel until dry. Put in a bowl with the bacon and mushroom mixture and parsley, then mix well to combine. Season to taste.

Melt half of the butter in a frying pan. Add the celeriac and mushroom mixture, slightly flatten it, then cook for 7 minutes until lightly golden. Slide out on to a plate, add the remaining butter to the pan and, when melted, tip the cake back into the pan, uncooked-side down. Cook for 10 minutes or until the celeriac is completely tender. Turn out on to a warmed plate and cut into wedges to serve.

This can be reheated in the oven for about 15 minutes if you prefer to serve it warm. Try to use pears of roughly the same size so you can arrange them neatly.

Pear tarte tatin

SERVES 4–6

225 g (8 oz) ready-made puff pastry, thawed
   if frozen
plain flour, for dusting
550 g (2¹/₄ lb) firm ripe pears

grated rind and juice 1 large lemon
100 g (4 oz) unsalted butter, at room temperature
175 g (6 oz) caster sugar
pinch ground cinnamon
clotted cream, to serve

Preheat the oven to 200°C/400°F/Gas 6. You need a 25 cm (10 in) heavy-based ovenproof frying pan, tarte tatin mould or shallow cake tin (not a loose-based one). Roll out the pastry on a lightly floured surface to a circle, 2.5 cm (1 in) larger all round than the pan, and about 3 mm (¹/₈ in) thick – no thicker than 5 mm (¹/₄ in) or it will not cook properly. Place the pastry on a baking sheet lined with parchment paper and chill for at least 30 minutes.

Meanwhile, peel, core and halve the pears and toss them in half of the lemon juice. Using a spatula, spread the butter evenly into the frying pan, tarte tatin mould or cake tin. Sprinkle over the caster sugar in an even layer and then arrange the pear halves, cut-side up, tightly together in the bottom of the pan. Cook for about 15 minutes or until the pears are caramelized and light golden brown. Remove from the heat, then sprinkle the pears with the cinnamon, lemon rind and the remaining lemon juice. Leave to cool a little.

Lay the chilled pastry sheet over the top of the pears, tucking in the edges and turning them down so that when the tarte is turned out, the edges will create a rim that will hold in the caramel and pear juices. Bake in the oven for 25–30 minutes until the pastry is golden brown and the pears are completely tender but still holding their shape.

Leave the tarte in the tin for a minute or two, then loosen the edges with a round-bladed knife and invert on to a flat plate. Use a palette knife to rearrange any pears that have moved, then leave to cool, if time allows. This enables all the juices to be reabsorbed and allows the caramel to set slightly because of the pectin in the pears. Cut into slices and serve on warmed plates with lashings of clotted cream.

afternoon tea

Teatime Treats

Perfect scones

Black forest gateau

Apple pie with a twist

Lemon tart

Piece of Cake

Cinnamon crumble cake

*Courgette cake with
orange mascarpone*

*Flourless rum
'n' raisin cake*

Summer fruit gateau

Sticky Fingers

Cherry muffins

Banana bread

Gingerbread men

Perfect scones

450 g (1 lb) plain flour, plus extra for dusting
1 tsp salt
1 tsp bicarbonate of soda or baking powder
1 tsp caster sugar
25 g (1 oz) butter

250 ml (9 fl oz) buttermilk
1 egg, beaten, or 50 ml (2 fl oz) double cream
clotted cream and strawberry jam, to serve
  (optional)

Sift the flour into a bowl with the salt and bicarbonate of soda or baking powder. Stir in the sugar and then, using your fingertips, rub in the butter until the mixture resembles fine breadcrumbs.

Make a well in the centre and pour in the buttermilk and beaten egg or cream. Using a tablespoon, gently and quickly stir the liquid into the flour. It should be soft but not sticky.

Lightly flour the work surface. Turn the dough out onto it and pat into a circle about 2.5 cm (1 in) thick. Cut into triangles with a sharp knife or stamp out 5 cm (2 in) rounds with a cutter. Arrange on a non-stick baking sheet and bake for 15 minutes until well risen and golden brown. Leave to cool for at least 10 minutes on a wire rack, then serve with the clotted cream and jam, if liked.

Nutty

Use half granary malted flour and half plain flour, then add 1–2 tablespoons finely chopped nuts or toasted sesame seeds or pinhead oatmeal to the mix before adding the buttermilk.

Cheddar

Mix 25 g (1 oz) grated mature Cheddar in with the buttermilk. Brush the finished scones with melted butter and sprinkle with another 85 g (3 oz) grated mature Cheddar before baking. Mix 1 teaspoon wholegrain mustard into 25 g (1 oz) butter and use to spread on the split baked scones before topping with hand-carved cooked ham to serve.

Fruit

Add 50 g (2 oz) sultanas or raisins or dried pitted cherries when stirring the sugar into the dry ingredients, then finish as described above.

This is perfect for a special afternoon tea.

Black forest gateau

SERVES 6–8

250 g (9 oz) self-raising flour, plus extra for dusting

100 g (4 oz) cocoa powder

350 g (12 oz) butter, at room temperature, plus extra for greasing

350 g (12 oz) golden caster sugar

6 eggs

2 × 400 g (14 oz) cans black cherries in syrup

2 tbsp kirsch

600 ml (1 pint) double cream

250 g (9 oz) plain chocolate

Preheat the oven to 160°C/325°F/Gas 3. Lightly butter a 20 cm (8 in) loose-bottomed cake tin, then dust with a little plain flour and shake off the excess; alternatively, line the tin with parchment paper.

Sift the flour and cocoa powder into a bowl. Place the butter and sugar in a separate bowl and whisk until light and fluffy. Beat in the eggs one at a time and then fold in the sifted flour and cocoa powder. Transfer the mixture to the cake tin, level the surface and bake for 35–40 minutes until firm and springy to the touch, and a fine metal skewer, when inserted, comes out clean. Remove from the oven and leave to cool in the tin for 5 minutes, then turn out on to a wire rack.

Drain the cans of cherries and reserve 200 ml (7 fl oz) of the cherry syrup. Stir the kirsch into the syrup. Using a large serrated knife, slice the cake horizontally into three equal rounds. Arrange, cut-side up, and spoon over the cherry syrup mixture. Leave for 5 minutes to soak in.

To make the icing, heat 200 ml (7 fl oz) of the cream in a small pan to scalding point. Break 200 g (7 oz) of the chocolate into pieces and add to the hot cream. Remove from the heat and stir gently until the chocolate has melted and the icing is smooth. Transfer to a bowl and place in the fridge to cool down completely, stirring from time to time to prevent a skin forming. The icing will thicken slightly.

Whip the remaining double cream until thick and soft peaks have formed. Spread the bottom cake layer with half of the cream and cover with half of the cherries, pressing them down lightly. Cover with the second layer of cake and repeat the layers of cream and cherries. Cover with the top layer of cake and gently press the whole cake down.

Remove the chocolate icing from the fridge and give it a good stir. Using a palette knife, thickly spread the top and sides of the cake with the icing. Leave the cake to set in a cool place, then pare over the remaining chocolate, using a vegetable peeler. To serve, cut into slices.

This pie is really simple. Prepare with good old Bramley apples, bake in the oven for 20 minutes and voilà – apple tart. Serve with some Calvados custard, which can be easily made by stirring two tablespoons of Calvados into a carton of ready-made custard. Alternatively, heat a ladle full of Calvados over the gas flame of a hob until it burns, then drizzle over the apple pie – delicious.

Apple pie with a twist

SERVES 6–8

8 Bramley apples, about 1.25 kg (2¹/₂ lb)
juice 1 lemon
50 g (2 oz) unsalted butter
50 g (2 oz) caster sugar
375 g (13 oz) packet ready-made rolled

puff pastry, thawed if frozen
plain flour, for dusting
beaten egg, to glaze
1–2 tbsp sifted icing sugar
Calvados custard, to serve (optional;
  see above)

Peel, core and cut each apple in half, then place in a bowl with the lemon juice and pour in enough water to cover. Melt half the butter in a pan and add half the apples, then cover and simmer gently for 20 minutes, stirring occasionally. Remove the lid and beat in the caster sugar until you have achieved a smooth purée. Take off the heat and leave to cool completely.

Roll the pastry a little thinner on a lightly floured work surface, then trim the edges. Transfer to a baking sheet lined with parchment paper and chill for at least 30 minutes.

Preheat the oven to 200°C/400°F/Gas 6. Remove the pastry from the fridge and spread the purée over the pastry base using a spatula, leaving a 1 cm (¹/₂ in) border round the edges. Drain the remaining apples and cut them into thin slices, then use them to cover the apple purée in an overlapping layer. Brush the border with the beaten egg and dot the apple slices with the remaining butter. Bake for 15–20 minutes or until the pastry is puffed up and golden brown and the apple slices are tender and lightly golden.

Remove the tart from the oven and sprinkle over enough icing sugar to cover the apple slices, then, using a blowtorch, caramelize the apples (or place the tart under a very hot grill for a few seconds). Cut the tart into slices and place on serving plates, then spoon over a little of the custard to serve, if liked.

I always try to leave the filling for this tart in the fridge for the full two days to allow the flavours to develop before baking it. If you really want to show off, glaze the top of the filling by creating a wafer-thin sheen of sugar, as described.

Lemon tart

SERVES 6–8

7 eggs, plus 1 egg yolk
300 g (11 oz) caster sugar
300 ml (¹/₂ pint) double cream
finely grated rind and juice 3 lemons
175 g (6 oz) unsalted butter, diced

25 g (1 oz) icing sugar, sifted, plus extra for dusting
pinch salt
50 g (2 oz) toasted almonds, finely ground
225 g (8 oz) plain flour, sifted, plus extra for
   dusting
crème fraiche, to serve

Beat six of the eggs with the caster sugar in a bowl until well blended, using a wooden spoon. Stir in the cream and then the rind of two of the lemons (leaving about a dessertspoon) and the juice of all three. Pour into a jug – it should make 1 litre (1³/₄ pints). Cover with cling film and chill for at least 2 hours, though up to 2 days is best.

To make the pastry, place the butter in a food processor with the icing sugar, salt, the remaining egg and lemon rind, and blend for 20 seconds. Add the ground almonds and flour and blend until the dough just comes together. Place in a polythene bag and chill for at least 2 hours.

Preheat the oven to 180°C/350°F/Gas 4. Take the pastry out of the fridge and coarsely grate into a 23 cm (9 in) loose-bottomed flan tin. As this pastry is so short it is in danger of breaking up if you trying rolling it out. Quickly press the pastry up the sides and into the shape of the tin. Keep or discard any excess pastry.

Lightly prick the base with a fork in several places. Line the pastry with a circle of parchment paper and fill with baking beans. Chill for 15 minutes, then bake-blind for 12 minutes. Remove from the oven and take out the beans and paper. Beat the egg yolk and use to brush the base, then bake for another 8 minutes until lightly golden to form a glaze.

Reduce the oven to 150°C/300°F/Gas 2. Give the lemon filling a good stir, then pour into the glazed pastry crust and bake for 35–45 minutes or until just set with no wobble in the middle. Allow to cool, then carefully lift out of the flan tin. Score the tart into portions and dust with icing sugar. Lightly glaze the sugar with a blowtorch or under a hot grill. Cut into slices and arrange on plates with some crème fraiche to serve.

This versatile cake is best served warm. I like it with crème fraiche but it would also be good with clotted cream, vanilla ice cream or custard, or served with fresh berries or apple or rhubarb compote.

Cinnamon crumble cake

SERVES 6–8

100 g (4 oz) butter, plus extra for greasing
85 g (3 oz) plain flour
25 g (1 oz) cornflour
1 tsp baking powder
pinch salt
100 g (4 oz) golden caster sugar
2 eggs, beaten

For the Topping

100 g (4 oz) plain flour
50 g (2 oz) butter
2 tbsp Demerara sugar
1 tsp ground cinnamon
crème fraiche, to serve

Preheat the oven to 190°C/375°F/Gas 5. Lightly butter an 18 cm (7 in) square cake tin or a 23 cm (9 in) sandwich tin and line the base with parchment paper.

To make the crumble topping, sieve the flour into a bowl. Using your fingertips, rub in the butter until the mixture resembles fine breadcrumbs, then stir in the sugar and cinnamon. Set aside until needed.

To make the cake, sieve the flour into a bowl with the cornflour, baking powder and salt. Add the butter, sugar and eggs and beat together until well mixed and smooth. Transfer to the prepared tin and level the top, then sprinkle over the reserved crumble topping.

Bake the cake for 45 minutes until firm and springy to the touch. To test if the cake is done, insert a fine metal skewer into the middle – if it comes out clean, the cake is ready. Remove from the oven and leave to cool in the tin for 5 minutes, then turn out on to a plate and cut into slices. Arrange on plates with a dollop of crème fraiche to serve.

This is rather like a moist carrot cake and is perfect for using up a glut of courgettes. It's a good cake to get the kids involved with, especially if they're not that keen on their vegetables.

Courgette cake with orange mascarpone

SERVES 6–8

a little butter for greasing
350 g (12 oz) courgettes
175 g (6 oz) walnuts
4 eggs
250 ml (9 fl oz) sunflower oil
grated rind $^1/_2$ orange
175 g (6 oz) light muscovado sugar
175 g (6 oz) golden caster sugar
100 g (4 oz) wholemeal flour
100 g (4 oz) self-raising flour

1 tsp baking powder
1 tsp bicarbonate of soda
$^1/_2$ tsp mixed spice
$^1/_2$ tsp cinnamon
$^1/_4$ tsp ground nutmeg

For the Orange Mascarpone

1 orange
4 tbsp sifted icing sugar
250 g (9 oz) mascarpone cheese

Preheat the oven to 180°C/350°F/Gas 4. Grease two 20 cm (8 in) sandwich tins and line the bases with parchment paper. Cut the ends off the courgettes, coarsely grate into a clean tea towel and squeeze out as much liquid as possible, then place in a large bowl. Reserve 12 of the walnut halves for decoration, chop the remainder and add to the courgettes.

Place the eggs in a food processor or liquidizer with the sunflower oil and orange rind, then blend until smooth. Pour the egg mixture into the courgettes and walnuts, then stir in the two sugars. Sift the two flours into the mixture, tipping any bran from the sieve back in, and add the baking powder, bicarbonate of soda, mixed spice, cinnamon and nutmeg. Mix well together and then spread into the prepared tins. Bake for 25–35 minutes until well risen and springy to the touch. Leave to cool in the tins for 5 minutes, then turn out on to a wire rack and leave to cool completely.

To make the orange mascarpone, grate the rind from the orange into a bowl. Cut the orange in half and squeeze in about a tablespoon of the juice, then stir in the icing sugar until smooth. Fold in the mascarpone cheese. Use half to sandwich the cake and spread the remainder on top. Decorate with the reserved walnut halves. Cut into slices and arrange on plates to serve.

Your guests will love this cake. It improves with keeping and can be served for up to two days. I like it with a mixed berry compote during the summer months.

Flourless rum 'n' raisin cake

SERVES 4–6

25 g (1 oz) raisins

150 ml (¼ pint) dark rum

200 g (7 oz) plain chocolate, broken into squares
  (minimum 70 per cent cocoa solids)

200 g (7 oz) unsalted butter

4 eggs, separated

200 g (7 oz) caster sugar

1 tbsp sifted drinking chocolate
  (such as Green & Black's)

600 ml (1 pint) double cream

2 chocolate Flakes, finely chopped

Place the raisins in a bowl with the rum and set aside for at least 4 hours, or overnight if time allows.

Preheat the oven to 180°C/350°F/Gas 4. Line the bottom of a 23 cm (9 in) springform cake tin with parchment paper. Melt the chocolate in a heat-proof bowl set over a pan of simmering water or use the microwave. Melt the butter in a small pan or in a bowl in the microwave. Leave both to cool a little.

Beat the egg yolks in a separate bowl with half of the sugar until pale and fluffy. Beat in the melted chocolate, followed by the melted butter. Drain the excess rum from the raisins and reserve, then stir the raisins into the mixture.

Beat the egg whites in a large bowl until soft peaks form, beat in a couple of tablespoons of the sugar and then fold in the remaining sugar until the meringue is thick and glossy. Fold in the drinking chocolate until well combined.

Loosen the chocolate and raisin mixture with a couple of tablespoons of the flavoured meringue and then gently fold in the remainder using a large metal spoon. Spoon into the lined cake tin and bake for 35–40 minutes until well risen but still fudgy with a slight wobble in the centre. Leave to cool for 5 minutes, before carefully removing the tin.

Whip the cream in a bowl until soft peaks form and then fold in the flaked chocolate and reserved rum to taste. Pile into a bowl and serve with the cake so that your guests can help themselves.

a deliciously rich afternoon snack

For a special finish, mark a thick dusting of icing sugar in a criss-cross pattern using a round metal skewer that has been heated over an open flame until red hot, then decorate with the berries and add another light dusting of icing sugar.

Summer fruit gateau

SERVES 6–8
2 x 250 g (9 oz) sponge flan cases
600 ml (1 pint) double cream
25 g (1 oz) caster sugar
2 tbsp brandy
100 g (4 oz) sponge finger biscuits

350 g (12 oz) jar mixed fruit compote
450 g (1 lb) mixed summer berries,
*   such as small strawberries, raspberries,*
*   blueberries, tayberries and redcurrants*
icing sugar, to dust

Line an 18 cm (7 in) springform tin with a little oil and cling film. Carefully cut out the centre from both flans, using the bottom of the tin as a guide. Use one to line the bottom of the tin and reserve the other to use as the top.

Whip the cream in a bowl with the sugar and brandy until soft peaks have formed. Cover with cling film and chill for at least 30 minutes.

Cut the sponge finger biscuits in half lengthways and use to line the sides of the tin, then spoon in the fruit compote to form an even layer. Fill with the cream, gently pressing it into the edges so that it helps the biscuits stay in place. Scatter over half of the mixed summer berries.

Cover with the reserved flan circle and press down gently. Place a flat plate over the top of the tin and then carefully invert. Remove the springform tin, keeping the cling film in place. Place in the fridge and leave to set for at least 1 hour, but up to 24 hours is fine.

When ready to serve, remove the gateau from the fridge and carefully peel off the cling film. Dust with icing sugar and decorate with the remaining mixed summer berries. Bring straight to the table, then cut into slices and serve.

The trick to fluffy muffins is to fold the wet and dry ingredients together as briefly as possible until just combined; don't worry if the mixture looks a little lumpy. These muffins are best served on the day they are made.

Cherry muffins

MAKES 10

85 g (3 oz) dried pitted cherries
150 ml (¹/₄ pint) buttermilk
150 g (5 oz) plain flour
1¹/₂ tsp baking powder

pinch salt
50 g (2 oz) unsalted butter, at room temperature
85 g (3 oz) golden caster sugar
1 egg, lightly beaten
¹/₂ tsp finely grated orange rind

Preheat the oven to 180°C/350°F/Gas 4. Put the dried cherries in a bowl with the buttermilk and, if time allows, soak for 30 minutes. Line a muffin tray with 10 deep paper cases.

Sift the flour into a large bowl with the baking powder and salt.

Cream together the butter and sugar in a separate bowl until light and fluffy, then beat in the egg and orange rind.

Make a well in the centre of the dry ingredients and pour in the cherry buttermilk. Add the butter mixture and quickly mix everything together with your hands until just combined. Don't overwork the batter.

Heap the mixture into the paper cases, filling them about two-thirds full. Bake for 20 minutes until well risen and golden brown. Leave to cool for 5 minutes, then serve warm or transfer to a wire rack and leave to cool to use later in the day.

This lovely moist tea bread is a great way of using up over-ripe bananas and has the added bonus of good keeping properties: it lasts for up to 4 days, wrapped up in parchment paper and foil.

Banana bread

MAKES 1 × 900 G (2 LB) LOAF
100 g (4 oz) butter, plus extra for greasing
225 g (8 oz) self-raising flour
100 g (4 oz) golden caster sugar

3 ripe bananas
2 eggs
6 tbsp clear honey

Preheat the oven to 180°C/350°F/Gas 4. Lightly butter a 900 g (2 lb) loaf tin then line the base with greased parchment paper. Sift the flour into a bowl and, using your fingertips, rub in the butter until the mixture resembles fine breadcrumbs.

Stir the sugar into the flour mixture. Peel and mash the bananas and tip into the bowl with the eggs and honey. Beat well until evenly combined, then transfer into the prepared tin.

Bake the banana bread for 1¼ hours or until golden brown and a fine skewer inserted into the centre comes out clean. Cover loosely with foil if it begins to brown too much. Remove from the oven and leave in the tin for 5 minutes, then turn out on to a wire rack and leave to cool completely.

A real children's favourite. You'll need to have the correct cutters. As the dough is really quite resilient there's no problem getting little hands to help with the stamping out. A great way to spend a rainy afternoon!

Gingerbread men

MAKES 10–12

350 g (12 oz) plain flour, plus extra for dusting
1 tsp bicarbonate of soda
2 tsp ground ginger
100 g (4 oz) butter, diced and chilled

175 g (6 oz) light muscovado sugar
4 tbsp golden syrup
1 egg, beaten
handful of currants

Preheat the oven to 190°C/375°F/Gas 5. Sift the flour into a large bowl with the bicarbonate of soda and ground ginger. Rub in the butter until the mixture resembles fine crumbs. Stir in the sugar.

In a separate bowl, beat the golden syrup with the egg and then stir into the ginger mixture. Mix until you have achieved a dough that will come together, then knead on a lightly floured surface until smooth. Divide the dough in half and roll each piece out to a 0.5 cm (¼ in) thickness.

Using cutters, stamp out gingerbread men shapes and place them on non-stick baking sheets. Re-roll offcuts and produce more men. Decorate with currants to represent eyes and buttons, then bake for 12–15 minutes until golden brown. Leave to cool slightly, then transfer to a wire rack and leave to cool completely. Arrange on a plate to serve.

INDEX